KITCHENS

James W. Krengel CKD, CBD, IIDA • Bernadette Baczynski

Lifestyle & Design

PBC INTERNATIONAL, INC.

Distributor to the book trade in the United States and Canada
Rizzoli International Publications through St. Martin's Press
175 Fifth Avenue, New York, NY 10010

Distributor to the art trade in the United States and Canada
PBC International, Inc., One School Street, Glen Cove, NY 11542

Distributor throughout the rest of the world
Hearst Books International
1350 Avenue of the Americas, New York, NY 10019

Library of Congress Cataloging-in-Publication Data
Krengel, James W.
Kitchens : lifestyle & design / by James W. Krengel and
Bernadette Baczynski.
p.   cm.
ISBN 0-86636-590-7 (hardcover) . — ISBN 0-86636-591-5 (pbk.)
1. Kitchens.   2. Interior decoration.   I. Baczynski, Bernadette L.
II. Title.
NK2117.K5K74 1997   97-22424
747.7'97—dc21   CIP

CAVEAT– Information in this text is believed accurate, and will pose no
problem for the student or casual reader. However, the author was often
constrained by information contained in signed release forms, information
that could have been in error or not included at all. Any misinformation (or
lack of information) is the result of failure in these attestations. The author
has done whatever is possible to insure accuracy.

10 9 8 7 6 5 4 3 2 1

Printed in Hong Kong

To my father

Bill Krengel, whose passion for

kitchen design instilled in me the

desire to learn all I could and to

be the very best I could be.

JWK

To my mother

and to my good friends,

with special thanks to

Kathryn Larson.

BB

CONTENTS

OREWORD

The new sociable kitchen is rapidly consuming other rooms in the home—aspects of the dining room, playroom, living room, and study can all be found in contemporary kitchens. The reasons for this phenomenon are manifold: the rediscovery of the pleasure of well-cooked food, the disappearance of domestic servants, the arrival of sophisticated appliances, the shortage of time families spend together, the rise of hobby cooking, and more. The list, in fact, is exhaustive. I'd like to hope that some of my own ideas, particularly the "unfitted kitchen," are partly responsible for this transformation. An unfitted kitchen is planned as a series of individual

Peter Aprahamian

pieces of furniture, each one designed to accommodate a specific task. When I developed that concept in the mid-1980s, it was revolutionary because it celebrated a freer, more versatile way of designing and furnishing a kitchen.

This is not meant to imply that there is no science in designing a kitchen. Quite the contrary. But the magic of a sense of place needs to be balanced with well-managed, functional design. When ergonomic and utilitarian considerations provide the basis for making design decisions, more solutions are possible because the kitchen is guaranteed to work. Then the decorative elements, the aesthetic, and the means of raising the spirits, can proceed. Marrying function with a sense of comfort is good design, and the future of the kitchen depends, above all, on that principle.

I see an acceleration of the need for the sociable kitchen, and why not? It is certainly a highly civilized trend; enjoying the process of preparing food is, after all, an act of love. To participate in lively conversation, to drink a glass of wine, to listen to music with the sun pouring in from the garden, to cook, and to eventually share in the communal pleasure of eating—all these are the essence of the kitchen of the past and of the future.

Johnny Grey
Johnny Grey & Company

INTRODUCTION

Of all the rooms in our homes, today's kitchens are most representative of our lifestyles. For some families, the kitchen is a sleek studio for creating elegant or elaborate party feasts. For others, it is a cozy room to prepare simple family meals; for still others it is a comfortable space to gather and socialize.

Recent developments in kitchen design reflect the fact that this room has become the heart and soul of our homes. The role of the kitchen has evolved and expanded tremendously, incorporating functions of rooms typically associated with the rest of family life, such as the dining room, sitting room, and family room. Additionally, the modern kitchen often includes aspects of more diverse areas of the home, such as the study, office, even the nursery and children's playroom.

The kitchens presented in these pages have been selected from all over the world, and they represent the many innovative and creative ways designers have met the contemporary LIFESTYLE and DESIGN challenges of kitchens and cooking. The need for a sociable, functional kitchen reflects not only our pleasure in eating, but our love of company and family. As you sift through this collection, you'll become aware of a recurring and welcome theme—an effort to bridge the duality of functionality and aesthetics, a sincere desire to live in both a comfortable and utilitarian manner.

James W. Krengel, CKD, CBD, IIDA
Bernadette Baczynski

L I F E S

T Y L E

URBANE RENEWAL

Location:
New York, New York

Square feet: 500
Square meters: 47

Design budget:
$70,000

Photography:
Frederick Charles

In the hands of noted New York architect Larry Bogdanow, the open plan of this Soho loft—with the kitchen taking center stage—has become an urbane design statement. No overdesigned elements were allowed to interfere with the kitchen's invitation to socialize and participate in meal preparation. Highly textural Jerusalem stone on the walls, touches of lustrous copper and bird's-eye maple, commercial-grade appliances, and gleaming woods all create elegance without ostentation.

"We used authentic materials and clean lines to achieve the high functionality that the owners wanted," explains Bogdanow. Thus, an open and beckoning pantry, with its wine racks and abundantly stocked shelves, combines utility with beauty, while the kitchen counter welcomes casual dining at any hour of the day.

The loft's open space required specific design considerations and solutions. For example, as it is not divided by walls, the space had to be defined chiefly through lighting and material changes. Direct and indirect custom lighting reinforce the natural light, drawn from windows at either end of the loft. Existing structural columns couldn't be moved so were eloquently incorporated into the design.

Above The view from the counter includes an artfully arranged open pantry, which cleverly doubles as a wine cellar. *Left* Structural columns, banded with burnished copper, become part of the overall design of the loft and kitchen.

LIFESTYLE

13

Right In the dining area, a grill lives in harmony with a custom-designed table. *Below* Jerusalem stone and copper echo materials used in the kitchen. *Below bottom* A curvilinear bird's-eye maple buffet fills a niche. *Opposite* The successful integration of practical functions is evident in this view from the living area.

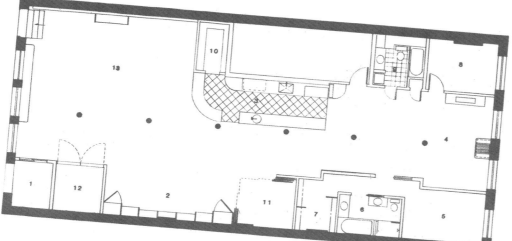

ECO-CONSCIOUS KITCHEN

Location:
Northern California

Square feet: 600
Square meters: 56

Photography:
David Duncan Livingston

When this California penthouse was built in the 1920s, little consideration was given to the cook's view. Letting in more daylight, as well as incorporating a magnificent view, were priorities when the present owners asked designer Agnes Bourne to remodel their kitchen. The couple, creative professionals who are active in the arts community, have a busy lifestyle that includes frequent entertaining.

Essential to making the kitchen part of the overall entertaining area was the creation of an open plan and new circulation patterns. "Now, the kitchen can be entered from the living room, dining room, and service area," says Bourne. "It has become the home's major nerve center."

Inspired touches, such as reflective surfaces to expand the room's airiness and subtle peach tones to complement the warm light, make this exquisite room an enduring work of art. But it is Bourne's commitment to sustainable design—manifest in the sturdy surfaces, energy-efficient appliances, emphasis on natural daylight, and recycling area—that make this kitchen ideal for the nineties and beyond.

Left **Brushed stainless surfaces offer a cool counterpoint to the kitchen's warm woods; ceramic floor tiles by Benedict Strebel of San Francisco blend both tones. For large gatherings, a buffet bar expedites food and beverage service.**

LIFESTYLE

Opposite The new floor plan's open arrangement is enhanced by a mirrored backsplash that reflects both sunlight and view.

Left In the breakfast area, small windows were replaced with a large picture window that opens the panorama to the entire kitchen. An island for food preparation allows two cooks to work side by side—and enjoy the view.

RUSTIC RETREAT

Location:
Southwestern Montana

Square feet: 298
Square meters: 28

Design budget:
$39,000

Photography:
Roger Wade © 1996

The rugged Montana wilderness is the picturesque setting for this spectacular vacation home. Designed by Kristie Eagle McPhie for an empty nester couple from the city that does a lot of entertaining, the kitchen was intended to be as bold as the view around it.

Since one of the partners tends to do most of the cooking while the other helps and cleans up, McPhie decided to make the most of the culinary partnership, designing separate cooking and clean-up areas, as well as an island that functions as an additional preparation area. With an eye toward the future, she incorporated ample turning room, roll-out shelving, and easy-care surfaces.

Left The eating counter is angled to allow guests to socialize with the cooks and take full advantage of the view. A rough-hewn log was fashioned into the bar counter.

The sensitivity of the design shines most brightly in touches that enhance the impact of the ageless view. Rimming the generous windows, natural plaster curves to meet broad panels of glass. The warmth of woods and the cool stone used for fireplaces and the home's exterior set the color scheme, while an absence of overhead cabinets and large expanses of glass keep sightlines open.

LIFESTYLE

21

Right Unpretentious and warm, the kitchen settles graciously into the great space. *Opposite above* Enkebol moldings on cabinets harmonize with formal displays of ornate antiques; a hand-wiped cream glaze adds richness to the finish. *Opposite below* Work spaces flank the cooktop; the bar in the background also functions for salad preparation.

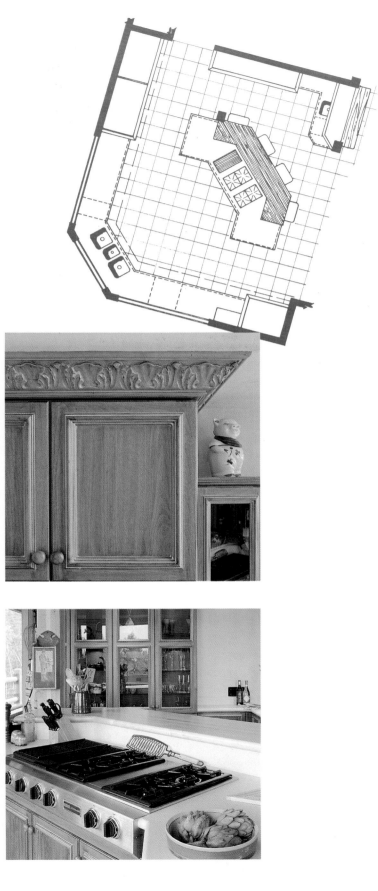

23

Location:
Huntington Bay
New York

Square feet: 400
Square meters: 37

Design budget:
$85,000

Photography:
Mark Samu

VINTAGE CHARM

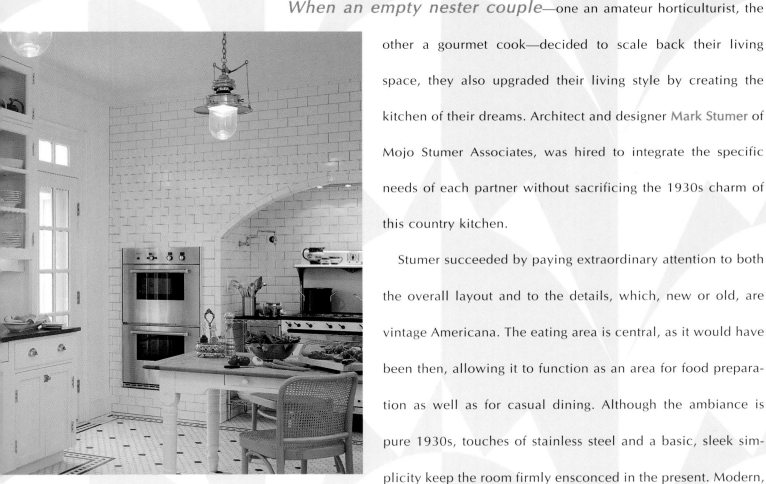

Above **Wood counters, a rustic kitchen table, and an abundance of sunlight warm up the glossy white surfaces that dominate the room.** *Left* **The commercial stove, framed in its own arched alcove, is the unique focal point of the kitchen.**

When an empty nester couple—one an amateur horticulturist, the other a gourmet cook—decided to scale back their living space, they also upgraded their living style by creating the kitchen of their dreams. Architect and designer Mark Stumer of Mojo Stumer Associates, was hired to integrate the specific needs of each partner without sacrificing the 1930s charm of this country kitchen.

Stumer succeeded by paying extraordinary attention to both the overall layout and to the details, which, new or old, are vintage Americana. The eating area is central, as it would have been then, allowing it to function as an area for food preparation as well as for casual dining. Although the ambiance is pure 1930s, touches of stainless steel and a basic, sleek simplicity keep the room firmly ensconced in the present. Modern, commercial-grade appliances meet the owners' exacting standards while blending with the kitchen's period design. Grounding the entire ensemble is an easy-maintenance, black-and-white tiled floor that is sophisticated enough to show off the room's enduring charm and functionality.

LIFESTYLE

25

Right The new drawer pulls and faucet coexist comfortably with a vintage toaster—adding nostalgic detail to the design. *Opposite left* A second sink for potting and arranging flowers is screened from the food preparation area by a low wall. *Opposite right* Mullion glass windows showcase the owners' collection of porcelain, pottery, and crystal.

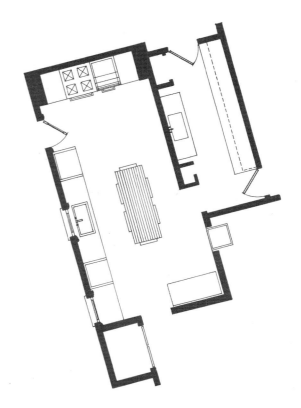

OLD-WORLD CHARM

Location:
Campobasso, Italy

Square feet: 288
Square meters: 27

Design budget:
$90,000

Photography:
Edoardo D'Antona

For this family, owners of a thriving olive oil business, a kitchen had to accommodate their needs both as food professionals and as a family that enjoys entertaining guests. Designer and architect Angelo Tartaglia skillfully blended their requirements in the creation of this efficient kitchen. "We did not want a very 'modern' kitchen," says Tartaglia. "We selected shapes and colors to go with the home's classical look."

The sculptural copper ventilation hood and brick fireplace are elements that give the kitchen a modified old-world quality. But Tartaglia has kept the overall design sleek, so that it never interferes with the room's elegance and functionality. As a work space, the kitchen is absolutely state-of-the-art. Lacquered cabinets conceal an extensive collection of modern appliances, including a meat-slicer and a rolling board for homemade pasta. In this way, surfaces are kept uncluttered to facilitate food preparation, and to welcome the array of family members and guests who congregate in the kitchen.

Above The cooktop, sink, and refrigerator are arranged in a step-saving linear sequence.

Left Double doors in the Art Deco style create a grand entrance into the kitchen and provide an elegant transition between the kitchen and the formal rooms.

LIFESTYLE

29

Below An additional dining area is located in front of the barbecue fireplace, which was also designed by Tartaglia. *Right* Flanked by glass-block windows, the half-round hood takes a dominant place in the room. A tapered pedestal supports one end of the island and reins in its large proportions; overhead lighting can be directed where it is needed. *Opposite above* Deep sills assume the role of display space for decorative essentials. *Opposite below* The backsplash, designed as an extension of the hood, repeats its graceful curves.

A CUSTOM KITCHEN

Location:
New York, New York

Square feet: 60
Square meters: 6

Design budget:
$70,000

Photography:
Everett Short

In New York's Ansonia Condominium showhouse, this tiny gem of a kitchen sparkles even in the absence of natural light. "The scant space necessitated a unique approach to the layout," says designer John A. Buscarello, "while the [imaginary] client's chronic arthritis called for sensitivity to the design."

Buscarello's clever plan decisively demonstrates that a small space can make a big statement. Cobalt-blue tiles, arranged in a matte-and-gloss checkerboard pattern, give the walls the look of a subtle texture, and warm cherry cabinets contrast dramatically with the cool walls and countertops. Avoiding the obvious, Buscarello accents the red and blue scheme with a surprising touch of celadon on the floor and ceiling.

The kitchen's appeal, however, is just as practical as it is visual. Open shelving, a push-lever faucet, and light-to-the-touch doors that can be opened with a fist provide user-friendliness. Appliances were selected for size, ease of care and operation; the under-the-counter refrigerator was installed at eye level. An inspired touch: easy-to-grasp coat hooks used as drawer pulls.

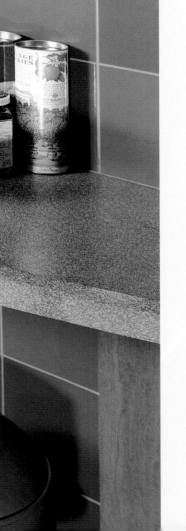

Left No sharp corners jut into the room from this gently curved breakfast bar. Above, glass doors frame open shelves which display a collection of dishes especially designed for arthritic hands.

LIFESTYLE

33

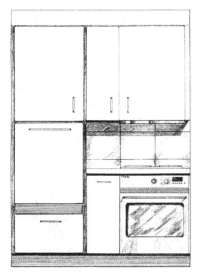

Right The geometric pattern of the linoleum floor ties the colors together, including the soft celadon of the ceiling. Wooden Venetian blinds have been stained to match cherry cabinets. *Opposite* The ADA-approved faucet features controls on top of the spout to facilitate usage.

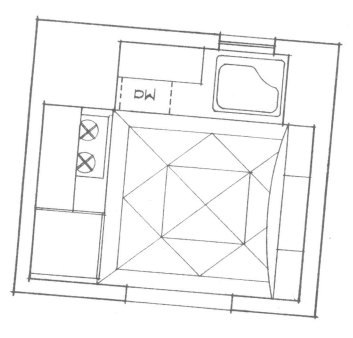

Location:
Central Florida

Square feet: 500
Square meters: 46

Design budget:
$80,000

Photography:
Everett & Soulé

GRAND SCALE

The owners of this opulent, Newport-style mansion are a couple who entertain frequently, often hosting charity dinners for upwards of 200 people. Rarely do designers approach a residential kitchen with an eye toward that professional degree of function and mobility, but designer Joan DesCombes and architect Roland DesCombes met the challenge beautifully. "In this home, kitchen staff and caterers must work together to serve large numbers of guests," explains Joan DesCombes. "Along with its functionality, the kitchen also had to impart the same sense of elegance as the rest of the home."

Designed as a professional kitchen, with state-of-the-art appliances and fixtures throughout, the space also incorporates residential touches. Elaborately designed European tiles and expansive displays of silver and crystal reiterate the home's lavish style, in a context that is extraordinarily functional. For ease of maintenance, all the walls are tiled and all cabinets and countertops are stainless steel; a floor drain allows for quick cleaning of the entire space. By defining the capacious room in terms of function—a main working area, serving area, pantry, utility room, even an office and sewing room—the designers have ensured the success of their plan well into the future.

Above An expansive counter in the serving area meets the needs of the professional staff.
Left Glass-fronted cabinets in the pantry allow servers to locate their needs at a glance.

L
I
F
E
S
T
Y
L
E

37

Right The feeling of intimacy in the kitchen's central food preparation area belies its commercial capacity. Behind cabinet doors, specially fabricated stainless-steel roll-out shelves and customized dividers accommodate an array of utensils and cutlery. *Opposite* French antiques and a crystal chandelier harmonize with the view in the serenely elegant dining room.

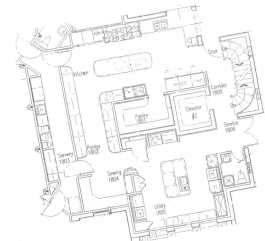

Location:
Westlake Village
California

Square feet: 660
Square meters: 61

Design budget:
$85,000

Photography:
David Valenzuela
Photography

CHEF'S SPECIAL

Family togetherness was the focus for Jane Brooks' design.

Above A single, horizontal row of blue-stained drawers adds a dramatic and unexpected unifying element. *Left* Wedgewood blue moldings on the cabinets' glass doors highlight the blue in accent tiles along the backsplash. Three sinks allow several cooks to participate simultaneously in food preparation.

A casual area was desired, where children, grandparents, and friends could be together while guest chefs cook. Fourteen diners can be seated around the table and bar, but many more guests can be entertained. Thanks to the designer's attention to circulation and flow, the owners have hosted parties for several hundred guests from this compact, hospitable kitchen.

The room's efficiency is indisputable. Appliances are state-of-the-art; refrigerator, sink, and cooktop are steps apart; a garbage disposal and additional sink make the center island doubly practical. But the kitchen also succeeds in the way it integrates appealing aesthetic details. Stairstep soffits lead the eye to display niches above cabinets; the granite inlay on the marble floor defines the traffic pattern and echoes the granite on counters; a strip of glass blocks over the windows by the sink creates a visual base for the shelf above.

LIFESTYLE

Right Essential to the kitchen's efficient design is its island, which is central to all cooking functions. Skylights illuminate the niches where the family's collection of pottery and primitive art is displayed. *Opposite* The hub-and-spoke ceiling defines the comfortable dining area without overpowering it.

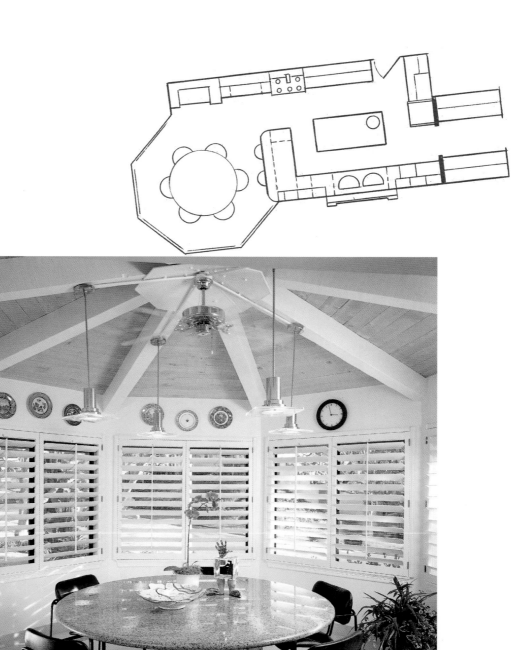

THE ROMANTIC IMPULSE

Location:
Southern Maine

Square feet: 395
Square meters: 37

Design budget:
$65,000

Photography:
Brian Vanden Brink

Designer Mary Douglas Drysdale believes that kitchens are primary spaces, on a par with living rooms. She has expressed that philosophy in this romantic, oceanside kitchen for an active, young, contemporary family. Their cottage off the coast of Maine required a kitchen that would work for meals with their two young children, as well as preparing dinners for 20 guests.

To create a space that displays the family's tastes and invites lengthy, casual gatherings, Drysdale employed a palette of brilliant whites and yellows, making the room cozy and warm even on the grayest of days. The room's brightness and simple lines also show off the owners' antique collectibles to their fullest advantage.

At the kitchen's heart is a central island. Rounded at the seating end, it invites conversation between the cook and children or guests. Simple columns adorn the corners of the island and base cabinets, lending the space a surprising romantic flourish.

Above An old-fashioned, galvanized steel sink is in keeping with this charming kitchen's character. *Left* The central island provides an ideal surface for food preparation and can accommodate up to six diners. Old hooked rugs and plaid balloon curtains add warm touches.

L
I
F
E
S
T
Y
L
E

Right Ample counter space allows for this handsome display niche.

Opposite Three rows of open shelving on one side of the island hold decorative pieces of pottery and allow young children convenient access to often used dishes.

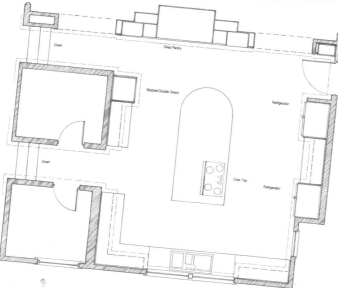

LIFESTYLE

EAST MEETS WEST

Location:
New York, New York

Square feet: 130
Square meters: 12

Design Budget:
$65,000

Photography:
Langdon Clay

Located in the heart of Greenwich Village, this town house is home to a busy couple and their small child. The owners, both professionals in the fine arts, travel far and frequently for their work. According to architect William C. Petrone of Sidnam Petrone Architects, the family wanted "a self-contained haven where they could replenish themselves" after months spent on the road, and turned to their Japanese heritage for design inspiration.

Functioning as an island in the frenetic sea of urban life, the kitchen, which is open to the rest of the house, is central to the entire environment. As in traditional Japanese design, the garden is a prime focal point; in Petrone's enlightened plan, it was important to expand the view of the garden from the kitchen, and to allow for through traffic between the kitchen and garden. To maximize both light and storage in this 20-foot-wide space, extensive demolition was required and a skylight, which helps to illuminate the adjacent dining room, was added.

In order to integrate the kitchen with the interior and exterior surroundings, Petrone created a room where straightforward though understated materials and elements abound: clean, custom cherry and maple cabinetry, natural stone, stainless steel, and unadorned expanses of glass.

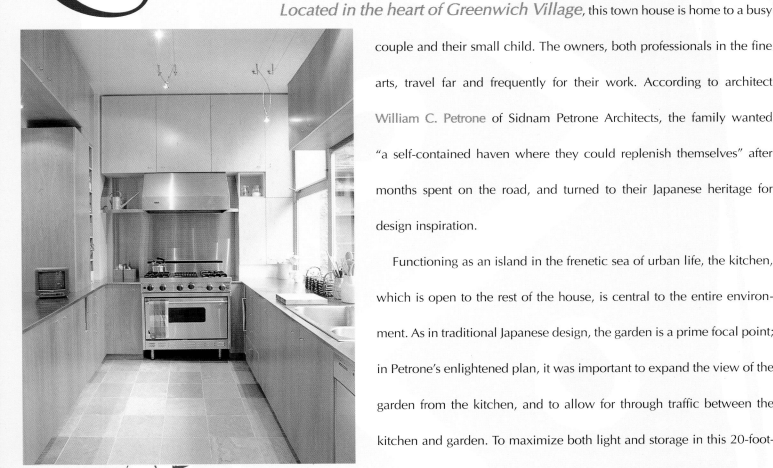

Above The softly variegated hues of the slate floor tiles subtly accentuate the slipped-grid motif that is repeated throughout the home's interior. *Left* Windows and skylight capture sunlight and expand vistas.

L
I
F
E
S
T
Y
L
E

49

STRICTLY KOSHER

Location:
Central Florida

Square feet: 325
Square meters: 31

Design budget:
$46,000

Photography:
Everett & Soulé

Many designers deal with the needs of two cooks working in one kitchen. In this house, however, designer Joan DesCombes designed a kitchen to accommodate the family's observance of kashrut, the Jewish dietary laws. As well as forbidding pork and shellfish from the kosher diet, these requirements prohibit the mixing of meat and dairy, as well as the commingling of utensils and dishes used for preparing and serving them. Consequently, kosher cooks have two sets of utensils, pots, pans, and plates.

To avoid the confusion this often causes, DesCombes' approach was to create a symmetrical design: two separate but equal halves—comprising both storage and prep space—to house both sets of cookware. Each half boasts its own inlaid granite cutting board, pantry, and roll-out cabinets. Food preparation and cleanup are handled with a sink of three compartments —one for dairy, one for meat, the middle for garbage disposal.

Although designed to observe ancient traditions, this kitchen is also state-of-the-art and comfortable enough to welcome the family's frequent guests. Amber maple shelving and cashmere-colored custom cabinets soften the room, and a spacious table in the center invites old-fashioned family interaction. Aesthetically and functionally, this kitchen serves more than a religious purpose; it makes keeping kosher simple and beautiful.

Above From the family room, the elevated kitchen's symmetry is clearly apparent. The island, which was lowered on one side to serve as a buffet, delineates areas without creating a barrier. *Left* Under-cabinet lighting and a convenient cookbook holder above the cooktop facilitate food preparation.

LIFESTYLE

51

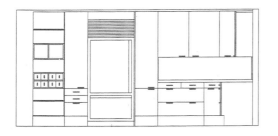

Right Encased in a storage wall, the refrigerator acquires a built-in look. Countertops are suffused with light from suspended fixtures. *Opposite* Maple floors and toe kicks are polyurethaned for gloss and durability. The diagonal lines of the flooring add a subtle pattern to the room's square design.

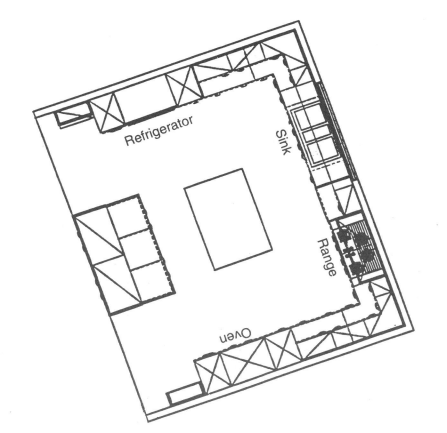

Refrigerator

Sink

Range

Oven

FARM HOUSE ADDITION

Location:
Lancaster County
Pennsylvania

Square feet: 175
Square meters: 16

Design budget:
$45,000

Photography:
© Andrew D. Lautman

In renovating her own 18th-century stone farmhouse in the Pennsylvania countryside, designer Mary Douglas Drysdale and her husband wanted a place to relax, entertain and spend time with their dogs and horses. The former kitchen and living room were opened into one living and dining area; the new kitchen space was created in a light-filled addition that exposes the rough stone of the original house on the interior wall. The use of a warm, monochromatic scheme naturally integrates the home's mellow antiquity with its quiet, sunny surroundings.

Drysdale's design is a stunning combination of rusticity and elegance, balancing elements of the two in unexpected ways. Bleached and sanded wide-plank floors and exposed rough-hewn beams coexist comfortably with Federal-period wainscoting, pediments, and furnishings. Most intriguing is Drysdale's decision to create three separate entrances to the elongated U-shaped kitchen. The functional benefit is access, but the aesthetic impact is a welcoming sense of spaciousness and light as guests are invariably drawn to join their hosts in preparing a simple country repast.

Above The luminescence of the custom cabinetry and millwork was attained by applying numerous coats of four different colors of paint. *Left* Shimmering pumpkin tones are enriched by the natural light that streams through the kitchen's only window.

L
I
F
E
S
T
Y
L
E

55

Right As seen from the living and dining area, the kitchen, with its meticulous display of collectibles, assumes the aspect of an art gallery wall. *Opposite above* A collection of blue and white plates lends a cool note to the kitchen's warm tones. *Opposite below* Access to the dining area and porch is close at hand.

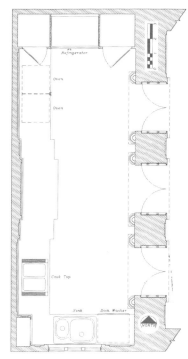

HUDSON VALLEY AERIE

Location:
Riverdale, New York

Square feet: 200
Square meters: 19

Design budget:
$45,000

Photography:
Wade Zimmerman

If this kitchen has the sun-dappled, pastoral quality of the Hudson River school, it's no accident. Architect Paul Jacob Hill lovingly crafted the design to correspond to its environment on those peaceful waters. As he explains, "We wanted to take maximum advantage of the romantic views yet make the space function for a sociable young family."

Certainly, the owners' need for a space where they can comfortably and casually entertain has been fulfilled, in large measure by the kitchen's center island—a focal point for cooking tasks. By intruding slightly into the dining room, the island accommodates the need for additional serving and seating areas. A raised wall at the island's opposite end shields the cooktop yet preserves sightlines to the panorama beyond.

In its details, such as the cherrywood cabinets that catch the glow of the afternoon sun, this kitchen is entirely consistent with the materials, scale, and charm of the 1926 apartment of which it is a part. It is, in Hill's words, a design that "lends dignity to the original architecture and moment to the new."

Left Structure and ornament are harmoniously wedded—custom-milled cherry posts support the carrying beam while playing a major role in the design aesthetic of the kitchen and dining areas.

LIFESTYLE

Right A second sink provides an extra preparation area. Forest-green countertops and accessories accent the verdant view. *Below right* From the stove, the cook has unobstructed interaction with guests. *Opposite left* The main sink was placed to take advantage of the spectacular outdoor vista. *Opposite right* A twilight view from the kitchen door dramatizes the Chateau-style architecture of the building.

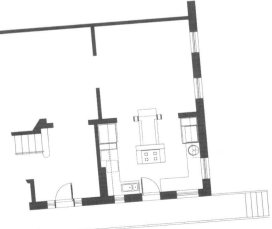

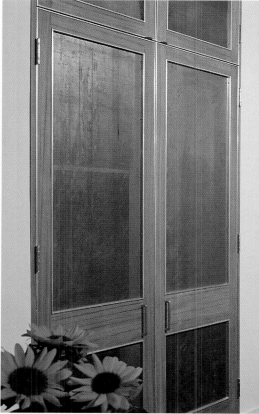

WORKING KITCHEN

Location:
New York, New York

Square feet: 420
Square meters: 39

Design budget:
$60,000

Photography:
Laura Resen

Above Lead-paneled doors conceal the laundry closet. In addition to their aesthetic interest, the doors buffer noise generated by the washer and dryer. *Left* Glass mosaic floor tiles define the kitchen's perimeter, offering an attractive surface that is easy to clean. The pattern repeats itself on the wall behind the stove and as an oversized backsplash behind the sink.

For his client, a graphic designer who lives and works in a compact Soho loft, designer William Sofield created a kitchen that converts easily from home to office, from private to public. "Since one must pass through it to reach other living areas," Sofield explains, "we carved out a kitchen that would be enclosed while maintaining the loft's spatial flow."

In Sofield's plan, many elements serve dual functions—before, during, and after business hours. The multipurpose center island, for instance, is actually a flat file cabinet topped with marble—for storage, food preparation, entertaining, and work meetings. Open or closed, translucent sliding panels emit light from surrounding areas. When the kitchen serves as foyer, a concealed pantry and basic white and stainless-steel surfaces keep it subtly in the background. Bordering the mosaic floor tiles, walnut-stained oak directs traffic flow around the kitchen.

For all its sleekness, the loft displays one touch of whimsy. Sofield retained the ornate, cast-iron Corinthian columns, original to the space, which flank the stove.

LIFESTYLE

63

Opposite left Sliding panels open to let in natural light from the bedroom. *Opposite right* When closed, the opaque panels above the sink convey the sense of a window while screening the adjoining living area. *Left* Transparent glass windows adjacent to the ceiling offer a continuous source of light, enhancing the warmth of the kitchen's soft yellow walls and teak frames and countertops.

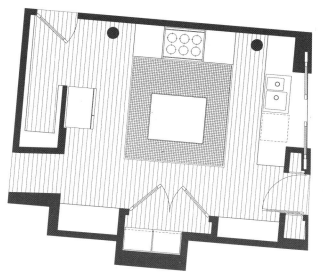

Location:
Campobasso, Italy

Square feet: 220
Square meters: 20

Design budget: $80,000

Photography:
Edoardo D'Antona

THE SEMI-PRO KITCHEN

Above Placed beside generous windows and a semicircular raised grill, the dining counter is an inviting spot to relax. *Left* An ingenious overhead lighting system mirrors the C-shaped work area and allows the cook to direct light precisely where it is needed.

In its timeless appeal and efficient planning, this is a kitchen for food professionals who enjoy entertaining family and friends in an elegant space. Designer Angelo Tartaglia created a C-shaped work area with the sink and cooktop at opposite ends and a generous preparation area in the middle. A dining region extends from one arm of the counter, out of the way of food preparation, but comfortably adjoining it.

By limiting the kitchen's color scheme to a sober palette of white, gray, and black, Tartaglia has allowed the food and the view to take center stage. In a particularly inspired design touch, unadorned black-framed windows display multiple vignettes of the view, which appear as landscape paintings that change with the seasons. In its linearity and functionality, this is a kitchen that will remain classic for years to come.

LIFESTYLE

67

Right The dining counter, which comfortably seats eight, overlooks the Italian countryside. Facing the walls with marble creates a unified surface that is also easy to maintain.
Below A rail for hanging items keeps mitts and utensils within reach.
Bottom The refrigerator anchors one end of the counter space.
Opposite A curved corner echoes the rounded edges of the counters.

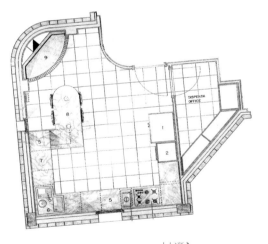

KITCHEN

Square feet: 260
Square meters: 24

Design budget: $45,000

Photography:
Maytag Appliances

FOR ALL SEASONS

At first glance, this attractive model kitchen's flexibility is not readily apparent—testimony that universal design need not be clinical—but closer examination reveals designer Jim Krengel's user-friendly, multifunctional approach. Such elements as varied counter heights, lowered storage units, and elevated appliances allow this kitchen to adapt to the changing needs of the people who use it.

"We incorporated more than 50 different features to meet different needs," Krengel explains. Some of these, like the trilevel center island, are immediately apparent, but more subtle touches include easy-grasp handles, touch-latch doors, glare-free lighting, and nonskid flooring. Even the most obvious departures from standard kitchen design, such as the raised oven and dishwasher, and the lowered, wheelchair-accessible cooktop and sink, blend seamlessly into the unified design. An angled mirror above the cooktop allows shorter cooks, or those who can't stand for long periods, to keep an eye on the stove, while taller cooks can work comfortably at the 42-inch-high counters at either end of the center island.

"Even if all the features aren't necessary today, they may be tomorrow," explains Krengel, "and that's what makes this kitchen ageless."

Above To eliminate unnecessary bending, the oven is raised an additional six inches off the floor. *Left* Cooks of any size can work side by side at this center island. At 30 inches, the island's lowest level is wheelchair-accessible and doubles as a dining area.

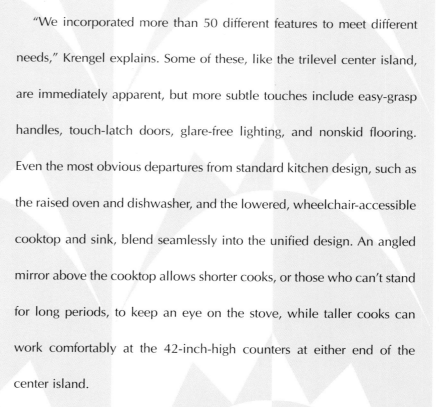

LIFESTYLE

71

CALIFORNIA HERITAGE

Location:
Pasadena, California

Square feet: 324
Square meters: 30

Design budget:
$70,000

Photography:
Grey Crawford

In this turn-of-the-century California home, historic charm and contemporary convenience coexist in harmony. According to designers Marc Reusser and Debra Bergstrom, the owners, a busy professional couple, and their teenage daughter are "pleased to live in a historic neighborhood and house." They wanted the kitchen to retain its old-fashioned quirks, yet function as a room for entertaining that flows easily into their garden.

Reusser and Bergstrom took a warm, neutral approach to the kitchen, letting the changing seasons and culinary activities lend the room its varied colors. They also oriented work areas toward the garden, providing unobstructed visual and physical access through an expanse of transom windows and generous French doors that open onto the patio.

The central island's massive size is mitigated through the artful addition of its gracefully turned legs, taken from a 1920s kitchen table. In the room's scale and detailing—flush inset doors and drawers, chrome-plated, period reproduction hinges and hardware—the designers have preserved the home's historic character, all the while remaining attuned to a modern family's needs.

Left The island is the primary gathering and preparation area. Substituting for overhead cabinets, tall step-in pantries are fitted with restaurant shelving for visibility and easy maintenance.

LIFESTYLE

73

Right Work surfaces are oriented toward the view beyond the French doors; a covered terrace provides leisure space between indoors and out. *Opposite* The faux-stone floor is a porcelain-bodied tile, highly stain-resistant and easy to clean. Tongue-and-groove paneling on the cabinet under the island adds a period touch.

Below Cabinets and windows are perfectly in sync with the home's historic ambiance. In the library niche, a built-in microwave oven fits below cookbooks and collectibles.

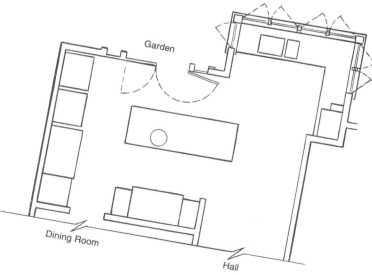

Garden

Dining Room

Hall

FLOATING ISLANDS

Location:
New Jersey

Square feet: 500
Square meters: 46

Design budget:
$70,000

Photography:
Peter Rymwid

Designer Barton A. Lidsky took this kitchen back to the basics with an artful arrangement of three simple geometrical islands, cleverly placed to personalize an expansive area. "A single island would have been too massive," explains Lidsky. "In this plan, each shape serves a specific function—rectangular for preparation, triangular for display, and circular for dining."

To reinforce their uses and infuse the space with drama, the islands are set at different heights, which makes them appear to float. Their geometric shapes are reiterated by ceiling soffits. Softening the room's impact are traditional materials like rich maple, oak, and mahogany that play off the stark forms and the coolness of stainless steel and granite.

The surprise, of course, is the ornate, eighteenth-century German hutch that dominates the room from all angles. "The owners told me they wanted to have some fun with this kitchen design," says Lidsky, "and we did."

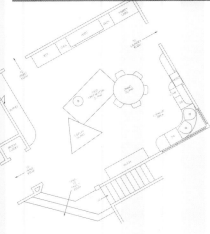

Above The rectangular preparation island is oriented toward the view of the outdoors as well as the circular dining island, where guests can comfortably congregate. *Left* The range's exhaust hood, the lighting fixtures, and the ceiling, which is dropped in certain areas, all echo the islands' geometry.

$\mathcal{U}$RBAN VILLA

Location:
Milan, Italy

Square feet: 180
Square meters: 17

Design budget:
$35,000

Photography:
Roberta Frateschi

Above As seen from the terrace, a glass-block wall creates an unusual and dramatic entrance into the kitchen. *Left* Blending seamlessly into the counter, the sink is positioned unobtrusively in a smoothly rounded corner.

The intrigue of this sophisticated kitchen is the ease with which it blends into its surroundings, a handsome Italian villa in Milan. For his clients, a young professional couple, designer **Angelo Tartaglia** created an exquisite, otherworldly space that has state-of-the-art conveniences with little suggestion that it is, indeed, a kitchen. This is achieved entirely by design. "We wanted a kitchen in which you would not immediately realize that you were in a kitchen," Tartaglia explains. "The owners' lifestyle is dynamic, and the kitchen had to reflect that quality."

A glass-block wall sets the tone for the room's unadorned surfaces and polished feeling. The design, however, is anything but sterile. Instead, the space is softened and made inviting by the curvilinear lines of the chandelier, the accessories, and the graceful, waving flow of the cabinets. It's a futuristic room that cleverly and compactly meets everyday requirements.

D E S I G N

83

Opposite left The cooktop is barely visible from the table. *Center* From an oblique angle, the curves of the cabinets are particularly striking. Bullnose-edged counters and tubular drawer pulls echo the cabinets' undulating form, while highly polished floors create the illusion that they are floating in space.

Left Jalousie windows are perfectly placed to admit the view and to enhance the architectural appeal of the glass block.

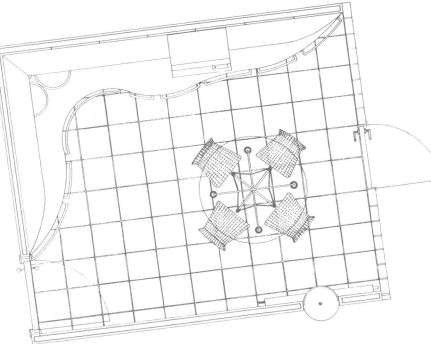

D
E
S
I
G
N

83

Location:
New Canaan
Connecticut

Square feet: 450
Square meters: 42

Photography:
Dan Cornish

ENLIGHTENED TUDOR

Above A single arched cabinet is an understated repetition of the kitchen's arches and vaulted ceiling, turning the cooking area into a focal point.

Left A butler's pantry adjoins the formal dining room. Although separated from the main kitchen, the pantry was designed to match the total kitchen area.

In the 1920s, this kitchen, a series of awkwardly connected, dark spaces removed from family activity, was the domain of servants. But in its modern incarnation, architects **Orr & Taylor (now Robert Orr & Associates)** created a timeless, classical design that has become the sunny heart of a gracious family living and gathering area.

First Orr developed a cross-axial sequence of spaces relating to the kitchen, directing family activities to adjacent casual-living spaces. To ensure that the area remained consistent with the rest of the home, yet without sacrificing efficiency, Orr kept the stylistic appeal of the Tudor design. He then lightened its impact with soft curves, a sun-filled breakfast bay with an inviting window seat, mullion-glass cabinets, artificial lighting that highlights architectural features, and an abundance of pure white.

Black marble countertops provide a stark contrast to the room's overall whiteness. The orderly sophistication of the black-and-white scheme is given an earthy touch through the warm spicy tones of Portuguese floor tiles that unite the various spaces in this appealing family kitchen.

DESIGN

85

Right A series of arches define the boundaries of the kitchen and breakfast areas, drawing the eye toward the view. A single vaulted window enhances the sense of perspective. *Opposite* An arched pediment on the far wall echoes the curved shape of the ceiling and leads the eye upward. The kitchen's clean symmetry is offset by the diagonal patterns of the backsplashes and floor tiles; the corner sink is oriented toward the view. *Below* The classic arches, paneling, and moldings in the kitchen are reiterated in the family room.

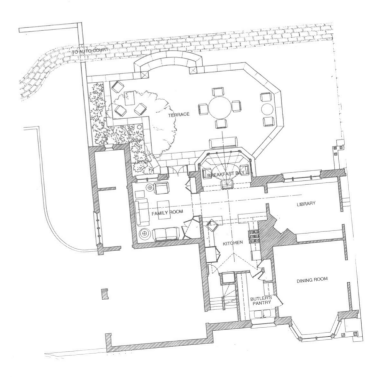

THE WARMTH OF WOOD

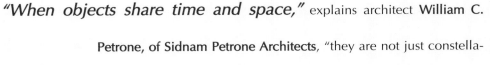

Location:
Saddle River, New Jersey

Square feet: 300
Square meters: 56

Design budget: $60,000

Photography:
Jeff McNamara
Reprinted by permission from *House Beautiful*, copyright© February 1997, The Hearst Corporation. All Rights Reserved.

"When objects share time and space," explains architect **William C. Petrone, of Sidnam Petrone Architects**, "they are not just constellations of material, but things 'being together' in the world." To create such harmony in this kitchen, Petrone designed a space that is spare in form and rich in texture—one that invites both conversation and contemplation.

What is most striking about this serene kitchen is its sense of "lightness." Petrone achieved the effect by sheathing the walls in honeyed maple veneers. The grain of the sanded plywood cabinetry shows through the clear finish, which, along with stainless elements like the counters and cooktop, reflects the wash of natural sunlight filtering through the trees. For all its perceived delicacy, this is a cost-conscious kitchen featuring extraordinarily durable materials and fixtures—slate floors, stainless-steel counters, and standard hardware—that are designed to last. In the cleanness and warmth of his design, Petrone has shaped a quiet space where natural materials and the beautiful view share the spotlight with the people inside.

Left This kitchen has ample storage space, but the built-in banquette provides even more. Beautiful and durable, the multicolored Indian slate floor provides a cool counterpoint to the room's warmth.

D
E
S
I
G
N

89

Right Directly facing the preparation area, kitchen windows look onto rolling woodlands. Honeyed maple surfaces, including a row of storage cabinets above the window, frame the view. *Opposite* The preparation area is both compact and efficient. The pass-through above the sink opens the room to yet another outdoor view. *Below* Table and chairs in the style of Charles and Ray Eames lend a 1950s retro touch.

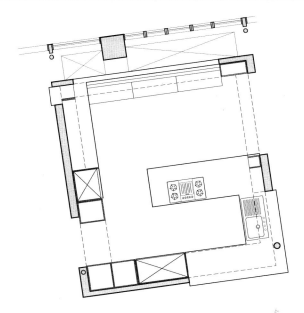

A SOCIABLE KITCHEN

Location:
London, England

Square feet: 600
Square meters: 56

Photography:
James Mortimer

Breaking ranks with traditional thought is the essence of any **Johnny Grey** kitchen. Designed for a young family active in London's food world, the kitchen of this Victorian town house in posh Kensington has cheerfully taken over the entire first floor, drawing a casual sitting area and a semiformal dining room into its generous proportions.

Grey created the center island, a sculptural element comprised of warm woods and hand-painted accents, to focus work activities "away from the wall, toward the room's center." Grey's preference for varied counter heights thoughtfully addresses the cook's comfort in performing different tasks: higher counters for the sink and preparation areas, and a standard-height cooktop. To reduce stress on the back, the designer raised the dishwasher 14 inches above the floor, where it rests atop a large storage drawer.

Grey's sensible ergonomic plan is ingeniously disguised in a warm array of rich woods, custom cabinetry, sensuous lines, and exquisite detailing, creating a room that at once surprises the senses and invites social interaction.

Above Convenient to the sitting area, a Portland stone hearth houses the family's extensive cookbook library. The huge cabinet, rear left, contains a freezer and provides additional storage for children's toys. *Left* A cherry drum cabinet forms the base for the maple preparation counter, which is accented with the delicate painted designs of artist Lucy Turner. Checkered bands of inlaid walnut and boxwood ornament the cabinets.

D
E
S
I
G
N

93

Right The view from the dining room reveals the scope and fluidity of Grey's plan. Chair fabrics and fire-place design details reiterate colors and lines from other areas. A handsome, cylindrical corner cabinet, with book-matched veneers and more accents painted by Lucy Turner, divides the preparation area from the dining area. *Opposite* Continuity of details and whimsical touches make the view from any angle a visual treat.

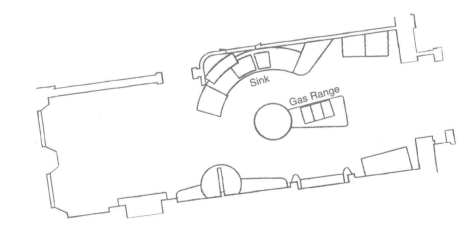

Sink

Gas Range

TRADITION REVISITED

Location:
Hewlett Neck, New York

Square feet: 600
Square meters: 56

Design budget:
$125,000

Photography:
Mark Samu

At first glance, this kitchen seems a study in contemporary design. A closer look reveals the subtle ways in which architect **Mark Stumer, of Mojo Stumer Associates,** married the disparate tastes of a couple; one who prefers a traditional look, while the other favors modern design. In meeting that challenge, Stumer imparted a timeless, welcoming quality into this beautiful design.

The room was extended to create the additional square footage needed to accommodate both owners' tastes. With its open floor plan, sleek black marble counters, and stainless-steel appliances, the overall effect is clean contemporary. Stumer deftly integrated the kitchen into the casual dining area and into the television-viewing and sitting area. The counter's end is curved to facilitate the transition between spaces, while pickled oak cabinets soften the black accents.

The incorporation of Arts-and-Crafts-style cabinet design from the kitchen into the table's pedestal base and on wall units, emerges as a traditional touch. Stumer allowed generous display space for such delicate touches as floral paintings and whimsical pieces of pottery. The intricate detailing of the glass-paneled cabinets is reminiscent of Frank Lloyd Wright's Prairie style.

Above By dividing the dining area from the kitchen, Stumer has endowed the space with a hint of formality. *Left* An unadorned wall of windows overlooks a traditional garden, while a large, freestanding hood establishes the island as the kitchen's central preparation area.

D
E
S
I
G
N

97

Right A bar sink adjoining the sitting room is separate from the kitchen's main traffic area. The cabinet wall extends into the sitting room to house the television set and a home office, a gesture that architecturally unifies the distinct spaces. *Opposite* Used sparingly, dentils over the cabinets repeat Arts-and-Crafts elements without overstating the look. *Below* The paneling and the base of the table eloquently reiterate the design motif of the cabinets.

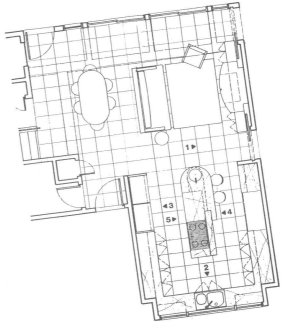

VANISHING ACT

Location:
New York, New York

Square feet: 120
Square meters: 11

Photography:
Andrew Bordwin
Sergio Jorge

Interior designer Bruce Bierman bases his work on fundamental elements: "clean lines, an efficient space, and a mix of contemporary and traditional design…more than any other room in the house, the kitchen must function". Appliances, storage space, and work areas must all be positioned to make the room as practical as it is beautiful. What better way to showcase his philosophy than by bringing clients into his own home, a New York loft that also serves as his office?

The adroit lines of Bierman's compact kitchen belie its ability to function efficiently as a space for both cooking and entertaining. The room's utilitarian character is cleverly concealed behind an imposing wall of anigré-wood custom cabinetry that extends as far as the ceiling. The cabinets are three feet deep—to provide increased cubic footage available for storage—and house a carefully organized system of pull-out drawers. Bierman even managed to incorporate laundry facilities in the kitchen.

When meals are served, the host can simply close the cabinet doors to hide food-preparation clutter. Once again, the kitchen becomes a spare, contemporary backdrop for a range of activites.

Above From the living area, the kitchen almost disappears into the larger environment, yet retains its bold architectural impact. *Left* Opened, the cabinets reveal masterfully arranged cooking and storage spaces. The grill, which conceals exhaust vents, spans the kitchen's width to create a strong horizontal element.

DESIGN

101

Right Black granite detailing complements the cabinets of anigré wood, a rich surface that is repeated throughout the loft. The island, which contains a double sink and cooktop, appears to hover above brushed aluminum columns.

Opposite In the dining area, sleek contemporary furnishings dramatically present well-chosen flowers and accessories.

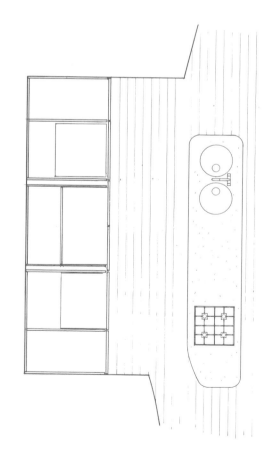

Location:
Westfield, New Jersey

Square feet: 225
Square meters: 21

Design budget:
$42,000

Photography:
Adrianne dePolo

Enlightened Design

Designer Ilana Vardi's scheme for this classic kitchen was to imbue it with light and drama through the creative placement of distinct window shapes. Although the room is somewhat small, a pitched ceiling maximizes the space. It also allowed for the installation of two quarter-round windows; architectural elements that are traditional to this 60-year-old, Colonial-style home.

For the overall design, Vardi retained other elements suitable to the home's style. Black granite updates the cherry cabinets, while their streamlined Colonial style, including a row of spice drawers, is reminiscent of a bygone era. In addition, an alcove that used to contain the range was converted into a walk-in pantry.

It is the window design, however, that integrates all of the other features. The quarter-rounds draw the eye upward, a triangular window blends into the pitched ceiling, and even the backsplash contains two glass-block insets. Over the sink, corner windows provide an expanded view and give the room old-fashioned charm. The abundant light emphasizes the stainless-steel and granite countertops, but most surprising is the way each window shape harmonizes in the small room, enhancing its particular environment.

Left The full visual impact and unity of Vardi's imaginative use of windows is evident in this view. Glass-block tiles integrated into the pattern of the back-splash admit natural light and add an element of surprise. A hexagonal sink is positioned beneath the corner windows.

DESIGN

Right Extending the backsplash up behind the stove creates a theatrical backdrop for the simple geometry of the hood. Above, a triangular dormer window eloquently restates the angle of the pitched ceiling. The granite-topped island provides additional seating without intruding on the preparation area. *Opposite* A detail of the backsplash reveals the intricate mosaic pattern—a miniature composite of the kitchen's palette of white walls, black granite, and warm cherry wood.

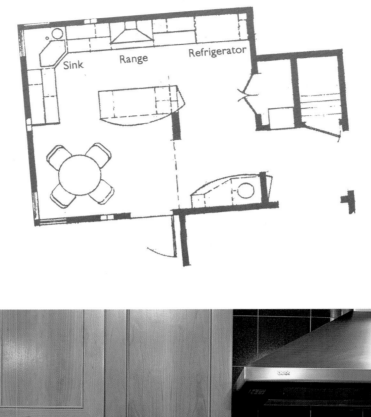

Sink   Range   Refrigerator

$\mathscr{E}$NGLISH ECLECTIC

Location:
London, England

Square feet: 1,000
Square meters: 93

Photography:
Peter Aprahamian

The greatest single improvement in kitchen design, according to designer **Johnny Grey**, is the central counter. "By placing a piece of furniture in the middle of a room," he explains, "activity is drawn towards the center." In this bright London kitchen, visitors are irresistibly attracted to the innovative island, which was designed to accommodate the activities of the ubiquitous, multi-purpose "working tables" found in most large English kitchens from the eighteenth century until the 1930s.

Matching surface materials to uses, Grey positioned the island's unique elements near the activities they serve: the cook-top is conveniently located across from the sink and refrigerator, the preparation area is beside the cooktop, the servery faces the dining area, and a low-level table provides room for small appliances, eating, and a children's work space. Overhead storage racks radiate from the stainless-steel hood, cleverly storing accessories directly above the areas where they are most needed.

"When you can see no limits to what is possible," says Grey of his eclectic design, "the results are nearly always better."

Left The unconventional yet sensible shape of the center island, with its distinct work stations was designed to allow for different activities, and served as the primary design inspiration for the rest of this colorful kitchen.

D
E
S
I
G
N

109

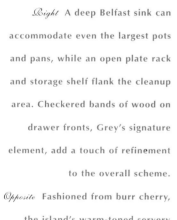 *Right* A deep Belfast sink can accommodate even the largest pots and pans, while an open plate rack and storage shelf flank the cleanup area. Checkered bands of wood on drawer fronts, Grey's signature element, add a touch of refinement to the overall scheme.

Opposite Fashioned from burr cherry, the island's warm-toned servery stands apart, both in its design and in its thoughtful placement near the hutch and eating area.

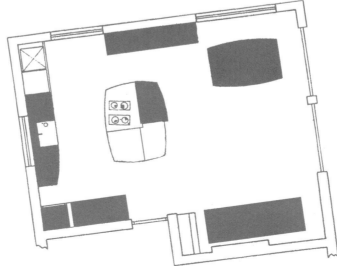

$\mathcal{A}$USTRALIAN STYLE

Location:
Warrawee, Australia

Square feet: 40
Square meters: 4

Photography:
Michael Nicholson
Reproduced courtesy
Houses magazine

Sydney architect Eve Laron's sensitivity to creating a space in harmony with its environment is evident in this lush kitchen set amid the treetops of southern Australia.

Part of the room's appeal derives from its lack of right angles—in keeping with the overall circular design of the house—which creates a dynamic sense of perspective that a square space would not have achieved. The room's oblique angles are also emphasized in the strong patterns of the various exotic woods employed, such as western red cedar and Tasmanian myrtle.

In the absence of windows directly to the outdoors, the kitchen is positioned to flow between the north and south ends of the home, letting in light and, most important to the owners, cross-ventilating the area. The kitchen's location on the home's upper level makes the natural, verdant surroundings uniquely accessible.

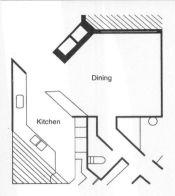

Above **Directly off the kitchen, a screened verandah is often used for dining. The counter facing the dining room works for either seating or serving.** *Left* **The kitchen is open to the living and dining rooms, and to a lush view over the treetops.**

D E S I G N

113

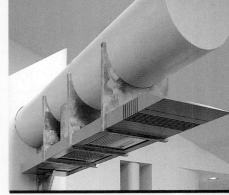

THE NEWS IN DETAIL

Location:
Kings Point, New York

Square feet: 700
Square meters: 65

Design budget:
$75,000

Photography:
©Jennifer Levy

Architect Mark Stumer's vision of the kitchen of the future is one that is "very practical, with large living and play spaces that are actually part of the kitchen." Stumer, of Mojo Stumer Associates, put his philosophy into practice in this kitchen, which he designed for an active young couple with three children and a large dog.

Above **The dining table echoes the kitchen's angles and curves.**
Left **Sunlight reflecting off brushed-aluminum surfaces creates ever-changing patterns on the walls. The design of the hood's support column reappears in the island's support columns.**

The stunning kitchen was detailed to be very contemporary with cutting-edge details. Its focal point is the hood, which Stumer fashioned to "float" above the quarter-round island. Its lines and surfaces are repeated in other areas of the room, so that while it commands attention, it also works as an integral part of the overall design.

Most unusual in this spacious kitchen is Stumer's choice of brushed-aluminum accents. On the table and in accents above the cabinets, on the hood, and around doors, the glossy material immediately draws the eye. Except for the granite countertops, the brushed design provides the kitchen's only surface pattern, thereby increasing its visual impact.

DESIGN

115

Right The centerpiece of the kitchen is its custom-designed hood, which in design and proportion takes on the appearance of a free-standing sculpture. The simplicity of its design achieves richness through the addition of brushed-aluminum details. A garden view is reflected in the oven panel.

Opposite Brushed-aluminum panels inserted around doors add texture in surprising places.

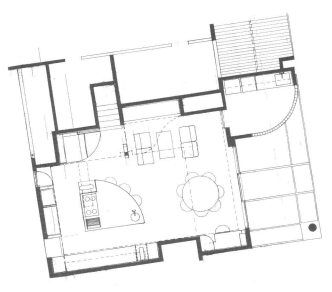

PREWAR PARK AVENUE

Location:
New York, New York

Square feet: 680
Square meters: 63

Photography:
George Mott

Above A separate area for quiet, intimate meals has been located by the staircase. *Left* The marble-topped center island, which is used for food preparation as well as a serving counter, includes ample storage space for trays, silver, and serving utensils.

In designing this elegant, urbane kitchen for an apartment on New York's Upper East Side, designer **Carl D'Aquino and architect Paul Laird,** of Carl D'Aquino Interiors, drew inspiration from the past. "We tried to create the feeling of prewar Park Avenue," D'Aquino explains. The kitchen now pays homage to the home's history in its traditional appearance, while its simplified layout and state-of-the-art equipment and appliances set this room firmly in the present.

In order to accomplish this duality, D'Aquino first demolished an assortment of smaller rooms typical of prosperous households of a bygone era, enabling him to open up the new space to meet the needs of a sociable, contemporary family.

The new kitchen can now be accessed from either the dining room, breakfast room, or foyer. These three entrances prompted D'Aquino to establish a very clear traffic pattern, which flows around a central island conveniently positioned in the middle of storage and preparation facilities. For all its modern efficiency, this kitchen still retains the mood and richness of a former time, with its lead-glass cabinet doors and accents, subtle Art-Deco lines, and traditional custom cabinetry.

DESIGN

119

Right Since the kitchen is not full height, the ceiling of articulated beams and moldings emphasizes the room's cozy appeal. Light shining through rippled-glass panes creates a shimmering display of crystal, while the striations on the Travertine floor tiles add a subtle pattern to the overall design. *Opposite right* This small niche is a welcome spot for sipping tea, reading, or catching up on correspondence.

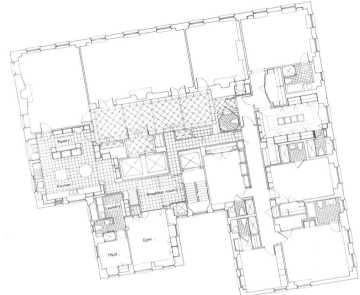

Left The diagonal pattern of the stone floor tiles, under-cabinet lighting, and reflective glass-tile backsplashes visually widen the room. *Opposite* A portion of the closet of an adjacent bedroom was incorporated into the kitchen to create this breakfast bar, which is recessed to open up one end of the space.

INDOW ON THE PARK

Location:
New York, New York

Square feet: 94
Square meters: 9

Design budget:
$40,000

Photography:
Chris von Hohenberg
Peter Margonelli

In this narrow New York City kitchen, designer Colette Whitney created a room in balance with nature while fulfilling the clients' requirement for a functional, open space. To achieve her harmonious design, Whitney selected a natural palette of textures and materials that mirror the kitchen's fortuitous view of Central Park. Warm maple cabinets, granite counters, and tumbled marble floor tiles artfully rimmed with mosaic borders reinforce the images seen through the window. Glass-fronted cabinets above a compact preparation counter open the corridor even further, directing the sightline outdoors.

When the view from the kitchen window is of Central Park, there's little doubt that the view must be part of the design. A practical application with a thoroughly aesthetic result is the narrow cabinet below the window, which creates not only additional storage, but a parkside window seat. Whitney also chose a simple, linen Roman window shade to allow the eye to focus on the view, not the window treatment. The additional lighting and the ease of movement and accessibility intrinsic to this kitchen make it a design that will endure for any stage of life.

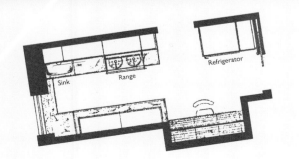

Sink   Range   Refrigerator

**D
E
S
I
G
N**

123

PURE GEOMETRY

Location:
New York, New York

Square feet: 225
Square meters: 21

Design budget:
$35,000

Photography:
Billy Cunningham

Architect Alexander Gorlin offers a decidedly futuristic take on the urban kitchen. "Since everyone in Manhattan works so hard and has no time to cook," he explains, "the kitchen will transcend its functional necessities and become pure sculpture."

Gorlin has attained that rarefied quality in this exquisite loft kitchen in New York's Tribeca neighborhood. The room is dominated by a triangular island, whose shape reflects the geometry of the industrial building in which the loft is housed. Stainless-steel counters and appliances glisten against subtle, matte black surfaces. The design is spare, streamlined, and thoroughly functional.

Yet the kitchen welcomes human interaction. It's an open, sun-filled space that flows into adjacent living areas. To make the kitchen family-friendly, Gorlin chose an easy-maintenance laminate that simulates the look of ebonized wood for cabinets and shelves, while a whimsical collection of Pez dispensers presides over the sink.

Above Radius edges mitigate the sleekness of the stainless-steel counters and backsplash. *Left* The triangular island is spacious enough to allow for storage, a wine rack, and seating for three. Matte laminate surfaces on cabinets softly reflect sunlight.

D
E
S
I
G
N

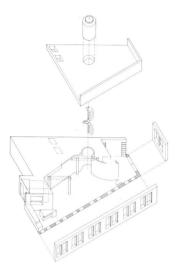

Right Counter seating was designed to be out of the circulation pattern between the living room and kitchen, yet part of the activity of both rooms. *Opposite* The kitchen's geometric impact is apparent from the living room. The positioning of the island endows the room with a soaring, aerodynamic feeling.

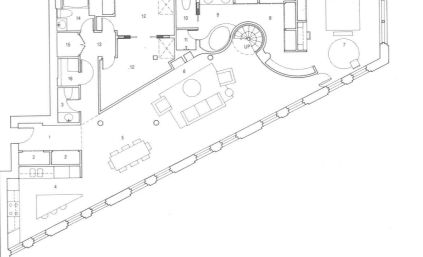

MODERN VICTORIAN

Location:
Bridgehampton
New York

Square feet: 150
Square meters: 14

Design budget:
$30,000

Photography:
Peter Ledwith

Above The centerpiece of the yard is an old linden tree surrounded by a flagstone terrace which leads to the front porch. *Left* The diamond pattern in the canvas floor cloth determined the motif of the custom marble backsplash over the cooktop. A cozy sitting area below the window forms an open foyer.

Since the kitchen of this 1800s house opens onto the home's only entrance, it was important to create a space that was warm, welcoming, and functional; it also needed to make an excellent first impression. Designer **Betsy Meyer** met this challenge by combining period details with contemporary appliances to create a kitchen in which antique design elements are featured for their aesthetic purposes as well as for their practical attributes.

Meyer highlighted the home's Victorian flavor and architectural features with crown moldings and old-fashioned cup pulls on the cabinets. Especially romantic flourishes are the bead board backsplash—with matching facings on appliances and exposed cabinet sides—antique pilasters, glass cabinet doors, as well as walnut-stained floors to complement the walnut Victorian furniture. Staggering the heights and depths of the wall cabinets to conform to the dormered ceiling creates two separate, symmetrical areas, accenting the room's idiosyncratic charm.

DESIGN

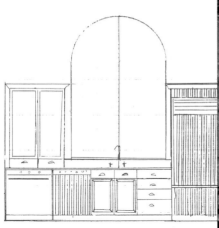

Right Upon entering the home, the eye is instantly drawn to the soaring arch above the sink. This opening allows light to enter the kitchen from the living room, but its major impact is aesthetic, since it displays a pair of antique wrought-iron gates. A Victorian marble-topped sideboard sits against the exposed-brick fireplace.

Living Room

Oven Sink Refrig.

Sitting Room

Kitchen

Covered
Porch

Lavatory

Bedroom

DESIGN

131

OPEN ACCESS

Location:
New Jersey

Square feet: 190
Square meters: 18

Design budget:
$40,000

Photography:
Erik Unhjem

For his own home, designer Barton A. Lidsky created a kitchen that invites family and friends to participate in meal preparation or simply to visit with one another. The open plan gently blends contemporary elements into a traditional setting. A wall was removed between the former kitchen and dining area and a curved peninsula positioned in between; its undulating movement is repeated in the narrow counter below the window. The visual impact of open shelving is softened with radius edges and an assortment of dishes and utensils chosen to enhance the kitchen's style and colors. Rounded sinks add yet another curvilinear element to the room's design.

Especially striking is Lidsky's ceiling treatment, which creates the illusion of a skylight within a dropped ceiling. The quadrangular light is positioned within a framework that subtly reflects the floor's diagonal marble tiles; wood moldings harmonize with cabinets and shelves. An unexpected and expansive touch is the deep greenhouse window, which increases the room's volume and adds a well-placed display shelf.

Above Open shelves effect a unique sculptural element. *Left* The design of the ceiling reiterates the pattern of the floor. Semicircular Lucite backsplashes above a single row of decorative tiles illustrate the Miesian dictum that less is more.

D
E
S
I
G
N

Right Lidsky took a singular approach to locating the microwave, integrating it into a storage wall alongside the refrigerator. *Opposite* The range hood, which appears more decorative than utilitarian, is cleverly joined with the shelf design. The hood's upper and lower layers curve inward to accommodate the exhaust pipe and cooking surface; the middle layer is convex, blending with the shelves.

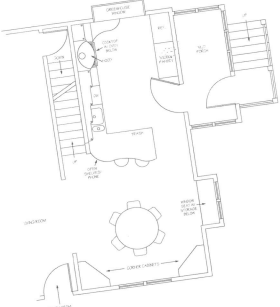

Location:
Central Florida

Square feet: 450
Square meters: 42

Design budget:
$50,000

Photography:
Everett & Soulé

ARTS AND CRAFTS

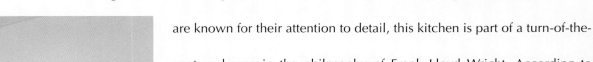

Designed for a couple who both work in the design industry and who are known for their attention to detail, this kitchen is part of a turn-of-the-century house in the philosophy of Frank Lloyd Wright. According to designer **Joan DesCombes**, the goal for the kitchen was "to reiterate the Arts-and-Crafts sensibility without making it too extreme."

To lighten the kitchen without divorcing it from its heritage, DesCombes reiterated the Art-and-Crafts feel while avoiding its sometimes overwhelming impact. White tile floors and simple white walls create a neutral backdrop for striking materials and textures. Elegant African mahogany on the cabinets, chosen for its consistently vertical grain, exudes richness, and although wood dominates the room, elements of brass and dark granite impart an architectural quality.

For all its grandeur, the kitchen is a functional, warm area to gather. There is abundant customized storage in the large center island, which is carefully placed to direct traffic past the main preparation area. Two sinks plus a centrally located cooktop on the island provide multiple work stations. The tall, white-framed windows offer a lake view that invites owners and guests to relax and enjoy the moment.

Above **A raised counter on one side of the island provides seating for four.** *Opposite* **By painting the oversized Prairie-style windows white, DesCombes has subtly incorporated them into the home's architecture.**

D E S I G N

137

Right Separating the casual eating area from the kitchen, a bank of see-through cabinets creates a double-sided display case for antiques and lets light filter through from both directions. *Opposite* Far Eastern flourishes such as an Oriental carpet are integrated with the Arts-and-Crafts-style window frames in the formal dining room.

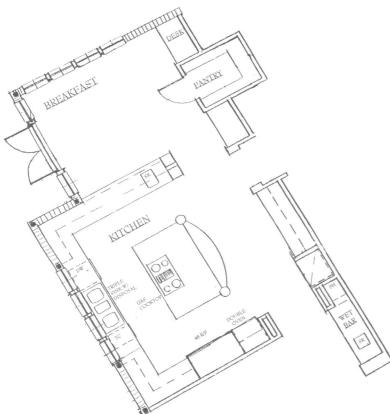

SIMPLE PLEASURES

Location:
New York, New York

Square feet: 100
Square meters: 9

Design budget:
$40,000

Photography:
©Wade Zimmerman

At first glance, the sleek elegance of this New York loft kitchen seems to overshadow its practicality. But its utilitarian beauty is the very essence of this successful design by architect and designer **Paul Bennett.**

Simplicity is the key word—both by choice and by necessity. The owners, parents of three young children, required unobstructed sight lines throughout the apartment so that they could monitor their children while handling kitchen duties. Circulation and access are controlled by allowing entry at only one end of the visually uncluttered kitchen, which has an abundance of storage space.

To make the kitchen the primary focus of the long, narrow space, Bennett concentrated color placement with a bold, simple palette of cherry wood, harmoniously complemented by a futuristic stainless-steel countertop. The L-shaped island makes the area's strongest design statement. "By using one low horizontal element," Bennett explains, "we provided lots of functional space while keeping the 'psychic' space of the apartment as open and free-flowing as possible."

Left The spareness of the kitchen's arrangement is evident in the placement of all appliances along one wall. Children can eat at the counter at the bar's end, in the area of the loft designated as a play room.

DESIGN

141

Right A grid pattern provides a potent design element in this home, imbuing it with a Zen-like serenity. It is repeated in the charcoal-gray slate floor tiles, the translucent walls panels, even in the artful arrangement of framed drawings. *Opposite* The recessed ceiling and square lighting fixtures define the formal dining area, provide a visual separation of the kitchen from the living room, and further echo the grid motif. *Below* A guest bath is centrally placed in the loft's design.

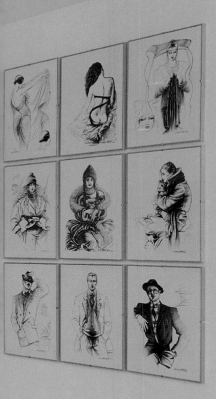

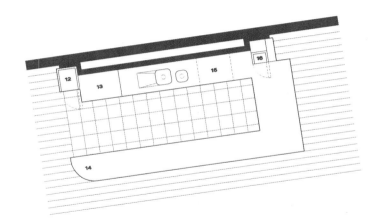

AN ANGLED APPROACH

Location:
Mahwah, New Jersey

Square feet: 395
Square meters: 37

Design budget:
$59,200

Photography:
John Schwartz

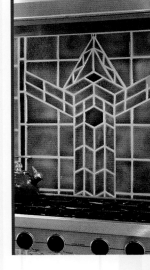

Angles prevail in this kitchen that Stephen Kinon designed for a busy professional couple. The repetition of the lines of the counters, cabinets, soffits, and range hood is masterfully understated, however, through Kinon's eclectic use of materials. He judiciously introduced fabric and curves in the counter seating, for example, adding just enough variety to soften the space without detracting from its drama. Pale-hued cabinets recede into the background, and, with the floors stained to complement them, the marble counters, preparation areas, and ornate tiled backsplash command attention.

The kitchen's focal point is the commercial stove, beautifully framed by a lowered counter, its stainless-steel hood, and the stunning design of the backsplash. Since the owners both enjoy preparing meals, Kinon has packed the kitchen with a range of appliances that allow serious cooks to be creative without feeling overwhelmed by technology. With all its exquisite detail, Kinon has designed a highly functional kitchen that exudes serenity and quiet.

Above The elaborate design of the backsplash above the stove is evocative of stained glass, and appears to support the visual weight of the hood. *Left* A warming drawer, double commercial wall ovens, and a professional cooktop fit easily into this kitchen's layout.

D
E
S
I
G
N

145

COLLECTORS' CORNER

Location:
New York, New York

Square feet: 104
Square meters: 10

Design budget:
$45,000

Photography:
Robert Blosser

When clients are enthusiastic collectors, their home must have adequate display space. In this instance, the kitchen is composed for such presentation. Architects and designers **Carol DiCicco Vinci and James Ahn** created a tiny kitchen gallery with ample display areas in this compact New York city apartment, allowing the collection's personality to shine in unexpected places.

Since the owners collect items primarily from the Art Deco period, the designers fashioned a cobalt-blue-and-silver color scheme reminiscent of the 1920s and 1930s. Every surface in the kitchen has a cool luster, elegantly encapsulating the polished mood of the era. Aluminum and glass shelving integrates the owners' ceramics collection and, just for fun, the designers specified custom, glass-chip terrazzo floors and countertops, giving the room a subtle 1950s touch. In this little gem of a space, all elements work together to make it feel bigger than it is, and to create a kitchen that is a showcase for collectibles as well as its own dramatic statement.

Left The consistency of stainless surfaces on cabinets, backsplash, and appliances—all durable and easy to clean—makes this small kitchen feel larger; the glossy ceiling enhances the room's reflective qualities.

D
E
S
I
G
N

Right To provide texture in a room of sleek surfaces, the back-splash is made of tufted stainless steel. *Opposite left* A small eating counter draws attention from the positioning of display shelves above it featuring vintage and designer ceramics. *Opposite right* A narrow, built-in buffet provides extra storage and houses wine racks at either end.

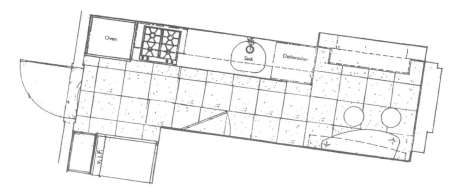

Location:
Connecticut

Square feet: 266
Square meters: 25

Design budget:
$50,000

Photography:
Lizzie Himmel

ARTIST'S GALLERY

Above **The breakfast room, a new addition to the wing, is glassed in on three sides and furnished with a 1950s kitchen set.** *Left* **A rotating selection of artwork above the fluted-glass cabinets comfortably coexists with the kitchen's varied surfaces and Art-Deco flourishes.**

Creating a kitchen that reflects a family's style and tastes is every designer's goal. Here, architect **McKee Patterson** has taken that precept to its ultimate end, fashioning a bright, open, and informal kitchen that abounds in unusual detail. The room's meticulous plan, which includes built-ins and ample storage for a variety of utensils, vases, and wicker steamers, makes it work for the family's everyday needs as well as for more formal entertaining.

Throughout, Patterson skillfully blends the warmth of an array of woods—maple, white oak, fir, and exotic padauk—with the unusual texture of fluted glass on the cabinet fronts and the sleekness of stainless steel, slate, white lacquer, and tile, producing a richly textured palette. Embellishing the whole are Art-Deco touches in the patterns of tiles and on inlaid floors.

The focal point of this very personal room is the band of 36 picture frames that lines the perimeter of the ceiling, allowing for an ever-changing exhibition of the work of the resident artist, or the children of the house.

DESIGN

NAUTICAL CHIC

Location:
São Paulo, Brazil

Square feet: 248
Square meters: 23

Photography:
Tuca Reinés

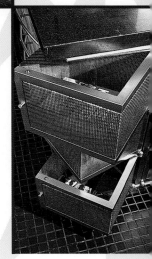

In this penthouse above the Brazilian clouds, architect **Arthur de Mattos Casas** designed a dramatically angular kitchen suffused with light, that serves the needs of a single-parent household.

A series of grids recurs throughout the room, uniting disparate elements such as the mosaic tiled floor, the recessed lights, and the shapes of display cabinets and storage bins. Overall, there is an inescapable nautical flavor to the plan. The round holes in the cabinets, which allow the client to view the contents of each compartment at a glance, are strikingly evocative of portholes. Drawer pulls are streamlined and stainless, their shape suggesting the curve of a ship's prow.

The natural wood grain of the cabinets adds a warm, random pattern to the design, while a stunning wall of windows lights every corner of this thoughtfully planned kitchen. The designer has kept surfaces sleek and simple, allowing the intrinsic qualities of the materials to shine through.

Above The counter houses a unique system of cubbies and stainless-steel swing-out storage bins. *Left* An extended counter separates the kitchen from the casual eating space, providing a serving counter for the dining room. A second sink by the dishwasher eases clean-up.

DESIGN

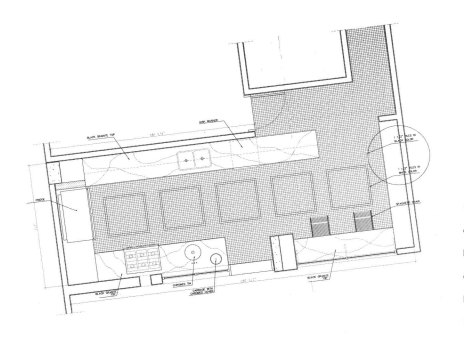

Opposite above The clean, nautical lines of the drawer pulls are complemented by the porthole-like cabinet windows.

Opposite below The eating counter doubles as a buffet for casual gatherings.

Center In this spacious kitchen, the main food preparation area has been compactly arranged. The extension of the floor tiles onto the toe kick makes the cabinets appear to float.

Left White mosaic tiles give form to the black expanse of the floor while simultaneously mirroring the grid design of the recessed ceiling lights.

DESIGN

155

KITCHEN BY THE BAY

Location:
San Francisco
California

Square feet: 80
Square meters: 7

Photography:
David Duncan Livingston

Above Nostalgic, 1950s-style boomerangs are appliquéd onto Mexican chakte kok wood cabinets, which are also adorned with ceramic tile insets. Countertops are granite. *Left* A yellow-stained center island offers generous storage space behind chicken-wire doors, a typically rustic material that Bourne has updated.

When designer Agnes Bourne turned her creative attention to the top floor of her own century-old San Francisco house—a combination atelier-den-guest suite that she appropriately dubbed "absolute heaven"—her approach consisted of equal parts playfulness and ecological awareness. Because the aerie overlooks the city's marina and bay, Bourne painted the walls with her signature faux clouds. As well as bringing the blue sky indoors, the walls function as a pleasing backdrop for the custom-designed furniture she either collected or commissioned from various San Francisco and European craftspeople.

The kitchen in particular exhibits Bourne's mirthful style at its best. Artfully integrated are myriad surfaces, styles, and colors that make this room a gem unto itself. Almost every element is nontoxic and environmentally sound. Bourne's commitment to sustainable design is reflected in her use of energy-efficient appliances and renewable timber sources for cabinetry and flooring.

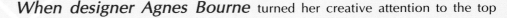

DESIGN

Right Aluminum reproductions of vintage office chairs offer a cool, utilitarian counterpoint to the capricious cloudscape. *Opposite* A corner space, fitted with shelving and handcrafted desk, is transformed into a viable work area.

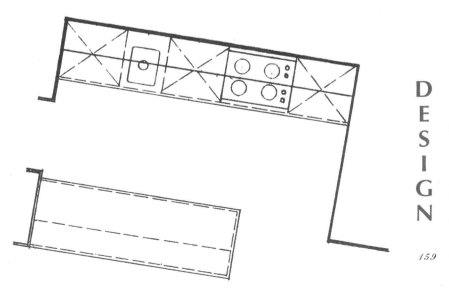

DESIGN

WHEN IN ROME

Location:
Rome, Italy

Square feet: 135
Square meters: 13

Design budget:
$40,000

Photography:
Edoardo D'Antona

In Rome, most people live in apartments. Kitchens are usually small, but, as architect **Angelo Tartaglia** has proven in his own home, limited space need not limit creativity. In addition to meeting his family's everyday needs and accommodating frequent guests, Tartaglia designed a kitchen that showcases both his aesthetic tastes and his professional work.

Avoiding the natural tendency to center the eating space in front of the window, the casual dining area is located in an alcove spacious enough to seat eight. Appliances are professional-grade and arranged so that the work triangle is efficient and compact, allowing the kitchen's architectural spaces to dictate their best uses.

"My opinion is that a functional kitchen should give you the opportunity to challenge your expertise in the art of cooking," Tartaglia says. With this unique marriage of technology and tradition, he has responded to his own challenge and created a comfortable, flexible, and distinguished space.

Above All preparation functions are concentrated in this linear arrangement, designed with concealed storage. *Left* A serving counter divides the eating area from the preparation space; storage is open and accessible.

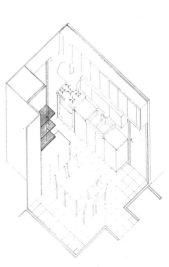

Left The efficiency and ingenuity of Tartaglia's design is apparent in this view. The kitchen's neutral palette directs the eye toward the terrace.

Right A glass door separates the
kitchen from the dining room.
Far right Metal cabinets with
translucent glass doors appear as
an extension of the backsplash.
The open shelf is within easy
reach, while overhead cabinets
take advantage of the area's
vertical-storage capacity.

GUIDE

The following 40 guidelines from the National Kitchen & Bath Association (NKBA) are not absolutes. They were established by the NKBA to create the most workable kitchens for the majority of users, which is the core belief of universal design. More guidelines might be useful, but these 40 are the basics. Dimensions are given with the idea that at any time, any kitchen may need to be wheelchair accessible. Guidelines that were specifically written to accommodate users in wheelchairs are marked with the international symbol (♿). Kitchens designed with these NKBA guidelines in mind should work well for anyone at any stage of life.

Traffic and Work Flow

1 ♿Doorways should be at least 32"(81cm) wide; counters which may flank a doorway should be no deeper than 24"(61cm) on one side. When two counters flank a corner entry, allow a minimum clearance of 32"(81cm) between the closest points of opposite counters.

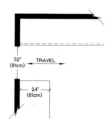

Walkways, which are passages between a wall or other vertical object and a counter or appliance, should be at least 36" (91cm) wide. ♿If there are perpendicular walkways, one should be at least 42" (107cm) wide.

Work aisles, which are passages between counters and/or appliances, should be at least 42" (107cm) wide in one-cook kitchens and 48" (122cm) wide in multiple-cook kitchens.

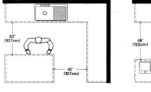

ONE COOK KITCHEN WORK AISLE

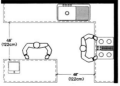

TWO COOK KITCHEN WORK AISLE

2 The work triangle is defined as the shortest walking distance between the refrigerator, the primary cooking surface, and the primary food preparation sink, measured from the center front of each appliance.

The work triangle should total no more than 26' (792cm), with no single leg being shorter than 4' (122cm) or longer than 9' (274cm).

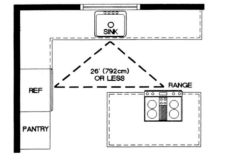

To insure smooth traffic flow, the triangle should not intersect an island or peninsula by more than 12" (30cm).

If two or more people cook simultaneously, a work triangle should be placed for each cook. One leg of the primary and secondary triangles may be shared, but triangles should not overlap. Appliances may be shared or separate.

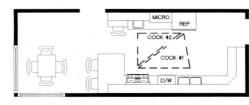

3 Major traffic patterns should be directed around, not through, the work triangle.

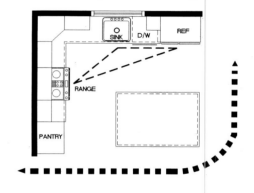

4 Entries, appliances, and cabinet doors should not interfere with one another.

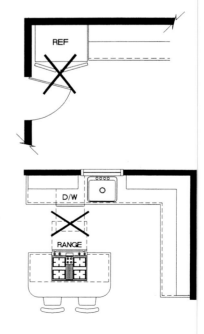

5 In seating areas:
If there is no walkway behind diners, allow 36" (91cm) of clearance from the table or counter edge to the wall or obstruction.

&If there is a walkway behind diners, allow a total of 65" (165cm) clearance, including the walkway, between the seating area and the wall or obstruction.

Cabinets and Storage

Wall Cabinet Frontage

6 In kitchens under 150 square feet (14 sq.m), allow at least 144" (366cm) of wall cabinet frontage.

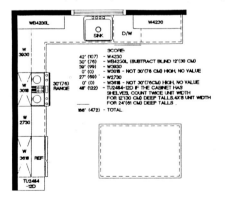

SCORE:
42" (107) - W4230
30" (76) - WB4230L (SUBTRACT BLIND 12"(30 CM)
39" (99) - W3930
0" (0) - W3018 - NOT 30"(76 CM) HIGH, NO VALUE
27" (69) - W2730
0" (0) - W3618 - NOT 30"(76CM) HIGH, NO VALUE
48" (122) - TU2484-12D IF THE CABINET HAS SHELVES, COUNT TWICE UNIT WIDTH FOR 12"(30 CM) DEEP TALLS; 4X'S UNIT WIDTH FOR 24"(61 CM) DEEP TALLS
186" (472) - TOTAL

In kitchens over 150 square feet (14 sq.m), allow at least 186" (472cm) of wall cabinet frontage.

In all kitchens:
• Cabinets should be at least 12" (30cm) deep and 30" (76cm) high, with adjustable shelving. Difficult-to-reach cabinets above the hood, oven, or refrigerator are not calculated in the frontage unless accessibility-improvement devices are installed inside.
• Diagonal or pie-cut wall cabinets count as a total of 24" (61cm).
• Cabinets 72" (183cm) or taller can count as either base or wall cabinets, but not both. Calculate tall units as follows:
  12" (30cm) deep: 1 × base lineal footage; 2 × wall lineal footage.
  18" (46cm) deep: 1.5 × base lineal footage; 3 × wall lineal footage.
  21"/24" (53cm/61cm) deep: 2 × base lineal footage; 4 × wall lineal footage.

7 Include at least 60" (152cm) of wall cabinet frontage, with cabinets a minimum of 12" (30cm) deep and 30" (76cm) high, within 72" (183cm) of the primary sink's centerline. A tall cabinet can be substituted if it is placed within the 72" (183cm) requirement.

Base Cabinet Frontage

8 In kitchens under 150 square feet (14 sq.m), allow at least 156" (393cm) of base cabinet frontage.

In kitchens over 150 square feet (14 sq.m), allow at least 192" (488cm) of base cabinet frontage.

In all kitchens:
• Cabinets should be at least 21" (53cm) deep.
• The blind portion of a blind corner cabinet (that area which is visually obstructed) does not count.
• Pie-cut or lazy-Susan base cabinets count as a total of 30" (72cm).
• Cabinets 72" tall (183cm) or taller can count as either base or wall cabinets, but not both. Calculate tall units as follows:
  12" (30m) deep: 1 × base lineal footage; 2 × wall lineal footage.
  18" (46cm) deep: 1.5 × base lineal footage; 3 × wall lineal footage.
  21"/24" (53cm/61cm) deep: 2 × base lineal footage; 4 × wall lineal footage.

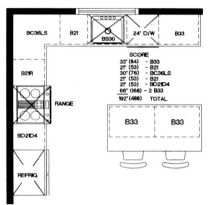

SCORE:
33" (84) - B33
21" (53) - B21
30" (76) - BC36LS
21" (53) - B21
21" (53) - BD21D4
66" (168) - 2 B33
192" (488) TOTAL

Drawers and Roll-Out Shelf Frontage

9 In kitchens under 150 square feet (14 sq.m), allow at least 120" (305cm) of drawer or roll-out shelf frontage.

In kitchens over 150 square feet (14 sq.m), allow at least 165" (419cm) of drawer or roll-out shelf frontage.

In all kitchens:
• Cabinets must be at least 15" (38 cm) wide and 21" (53cm) deep to be counted.
• To determine frontage, multiply the cabinet width by the number of drawer/roll-out units.

10 Include at least five storage and organizing items in the plan. &Items should be within the range of 15" to 48" (38cm to 122cm) above the finished floor.

Items may include (but are not limited to) lowered wall cabinets, raised base cabinets, tall cabinets, appliance garages, bins and racks, swing-out pantries, interior vertical dividers, and specialized drawers and shelves.

Along with drawer frontage, roll-out shelves may be included in the calculations requiring a minimum frontage of 120" (305cm) for small kitchens or 165" (419cm) for larger kitchens. *(See Guideline 9.)*

11 In kitchens with usable corner areas, include at least one functional corner storage unit.

12 Include at least two waste receptacles—one for garbage, one for recyclables—or include other recycling facilities.

The top edge of a waste receptacle should be no higher than 36" (91cm).

Receptacles should be easily accessible.

Receptacles should be removable without having to lift them higher than their heights. Most desirable: receptacles which can be removed laterally.

Appliance Placement and Use/Clearance Space

13 ♿When possible, include knee space (which may be open or adaptable) below or adjacent to sinks, cooktops, ranges, and ovens.

♿Under-counter knee space should be at least 27" (69cm) high by 30" (76cm) wide by 19" (48cm) deep.

♿To accommodate utilities, the under-counter knee space may be angled toward the wall as long as there is adequate knee space remaining to accommodate a user in a wheelchair.

♿For safety and aesthetics, surfaces in knee spaces should be finished.

14 ♿Provide a clear floor space, 30" by 48" (76cm × 122cm), at the sink, dishwasher, cooktop, oven, and refrigerator.

♿If the toe kick is less than 9" (23cm) high, measure from the face of the cabinet or appliance.

♿Clear floor spaces may overlap, and up to 19" (48cm) of knee space may be included in the 30" by 48" (76cm × 122cm) area.

15 Allow a minimum of 21" (53cm) of clear floor space between the edge of the dishwasher and any counter, appliance, or cabinet which is placed at a right angle to it.

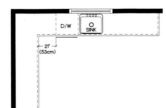

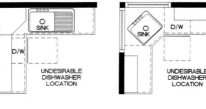

16 The edge of the primary dishwasher should be within 36" (91cm) of the edge of one sink. To accommodate other cooks or family members, the dishwasher should be within reach of more than one person at a time.

17 If the kitchen has only one sink, locate it between or across from the cooking area, preparation area, or refrigerator.

18 Allow at least a 24" (61cm) clearance between the cooking surface and an overhead protected surface, or a 30" (76cm) clearance between the cooking surface and an overhead unprotected surface. If the protected surface is a microwave/hood combination, the manufacturer's specifications may dictate a clearance less than 24" (61cm).

19 All major appliances used for surface cooking should have ventilation systems. Fans should have minimum ratings of 150 CFM (cubic feet per minute).

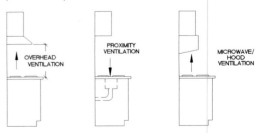

20 The cooking surface should not be placed below an operable window unless the window is 3" (8cm) or more behind the appliance, and more than 24" (61cm) above it.

All window treatments above cooking surfaces should be nonflammable.

21 Place microwave ovens so that the base of the appliance is 24" (61cm) to 48" (122cm) above the floor. To accommodate users with limited physical abilities, it may be necessary to place the microwave outside of the recommended range.

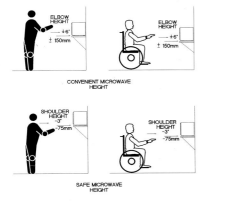

CONVENIENT MICROWAVE HEIGHT

SAFE MICROWAVE HEIGHT

Counter Surface and Landing Space

22 Provide at least two work-counter heights, one 28" (71cm) to 36" (91cm) above the finished floor, the other 36" (91cm) to 45" (114cm) above the finished floor.

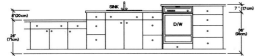

23 In kitchens under 150 square feet (14 sq.m), allow at least 132" (335cm) of usable counter-top frontage.

In kitchens over 150 square feet (14 sq.m), allow at least 198" (503cm) of usable counter-top frontage.

In all kitchens:
- Counters must be at least 16" (41cm) deep, and wall cabinets at least 15" (38cm) above their surface for counter to be included in total measurement.
- Measure along the front edge of counter-tops, not along the back.
- If an appliance garage or storage cabinet extends to the counter, there must be 16" (41cm) of clear space in front of it for the area to be counted as usable countertop frontage.

24 Allow at least 24" (61cm) of countertop frontage on one side of the primary sink (including corner sinks) and 18" (46cm) on the other. The 24" (61cm) countertop frontage should be the same height as the sink. The countertop frontage may be continuous or the total of two angled sections. Do not count corner space in this measurement.

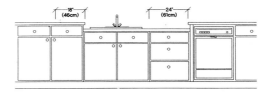

For the primary sink, minimum allowable spaces from the countertop corner are 3"(8cm) to the sink's edge, and 15" (38cm) to its centerline.

Allow 21" (53cm) of clear counter on the return if the dimension from the edge of the primary sink to the corner is less than 18" (46cm). *(See Guideline 31 for further information.)*

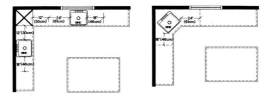

25 Provide at least 3" (8cm) of countertop frontage on one side of the secondary sink (including corner sinks), and 18" (46cm) on the other. The 18" (46cm) countertop frontage should be the same height as the sink. The countertop frontage may be continuous or the total of two angled sections. Do not count corner space in this measurement. *(See Guideline 31 for further information.)*

26 Plan a landing space, at least 15" (38cm) wide by 16" (41cm) deep, below or adjacent to a microwave. *(See Guideline 31 for further information.)*

27 In an open-ended kitchen plan, allow at least 9" (23cm) of counter space on one side of the cooking surface, and 15" (38cm) on the other, at the same height as the appliance.

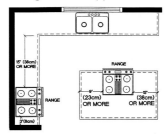

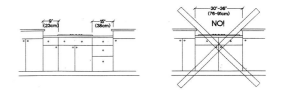

In an enclosed plan, allow at least a 3" (8cm) clearance at the end wall, and 15" (38cm) on the other side, at the same height as the appliance. *The end wall should have a flame-retardant surface.*

In an outside-angle installation of cooking surfaces, allow at least 9" (23cm) of straight counter space on one side, and 15" (38cm) on the other, at the same height as the appliance.

When cooking surfaces are on an island or peninsula, for safety the countertop should extend at least 9" (23cm) behind the cooking surface, at the same height as the appliance. *(See Guideline 31 for further information.)*

28 Allow at least 15" (38cm) of counter space on the latch side of the refrigerator or on either side of a side-by-side refrigerator, or at least 15" (38cm) of landing space no more than 48" (122cm) across from the refrigerator. Measure the latter distance from the center front of the refrigerator to the opposite counter.

It is acceptable but not ideal to locate an oven next to a refrigerator. For convenience, place the refrigerator next to available countertop. If there is no safe landing area across from the oven, this arrangement can be reversed. *(See Guideline 31 for further information.)*

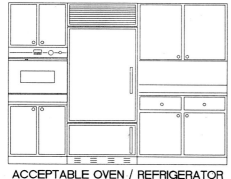

ACCEPTABLE OVEN / REFRIGERATOR PLACEMENT

29 If the oven door opens into a primary traffic area, allow a landing space at least 15" (38cm) wide by 16" (41cm) deep next to or above the oven.

If the oven door does not open into a primary traffic area, a landing space at least 15" (38cm) wide by 16" (41cm) deep, no more than 48" (122cm) across from the oven, is acceptable. Measure the latter distance from the center front of the oven to the opposite counter. *(See Guideline 31 for further information.)*

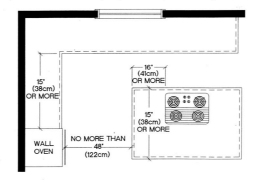

30 For the preparation center, plan a continuous countertop at least 36" (91cm) long by 16" (41cm) deep. The preparation center should be immediately adjacent to a water source.

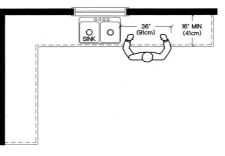

For preparation centers where two or more people work simultaneously, allow each person

a space at least 36" (91cm) wide by 16" (41cm) deep. If two people will work side by side, plan a space 72" (183cm) wide by 16" (41cm) deep.

The preparation center can be located between the primary sink and the cooking surface, between the refrigerator and the primary sink, or adjacent to a secondary sink that is on an island or other cabinet section. *(See Guideline 31 for further information.)*

31 If two work centers are adjacent to one another, determine a new minimum counter-frontage requirement for the spaces by adding 12" (30cm) to the longer of the two required counter lengths.

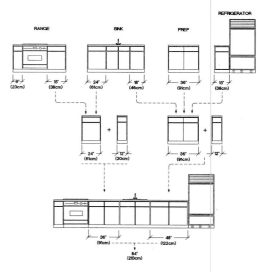

32 No two primary work centers (the primary sink, refrigerator, preparation or cook-top/range center) should be separated by a full-height, full-depth tall tower such as an oven cabinet, pantry cabinet, or refrigerator.

A corner-recessed tall tower between primary work centers is acceptable if knee space is planned on one side of the tower.

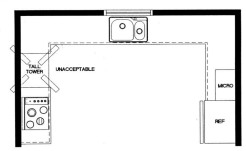

33 In seating areas, allow the following minimum clearances for tables and/or counters for each seated diner:

30" (76cm) high: 30" (76cm) wide by 19" (48cm) deep, with at least 19" (48cm) of clear knee space.

36" (91cm) high: 24" (61cm) wide by 15" (38cm) deep, with at least 15" (38cm) of clear knee space.

42" (107cm) high: 24" (61cm) wide by 12" (30cm) deep, with 12" (30cm) of clear knee space.

34 Open countertop corners should be clipped or radiused, and counter edges should be eased to eliminate sharp corners.

Room, Appliance, and Equipment Controls

35 Controls, handles, and door or drawer pulls should be operable with one hand, require minimal strength to operate, and not require

tight grasping, pinching, or twisting of the wrist. Such items include handles, knobs, or pulls on doors, appliances, cabinets, drawers, and plumbing fixtures, as well as controls and switches for lights, intercoms, and other room controls.

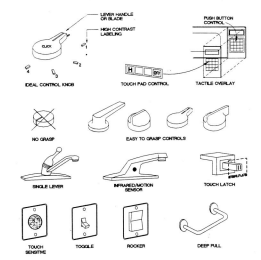

36 Wall-mounted room controls, such as receptacles, switches, thermostats, telephones, and intercoms, should be 15" (38cm) to 48" (122cm) above the finished floor. The switch plate can extend beyond that dimension, but the control itself should be within it.

37 Ground fault circuit interrupters should be specified on all kitchen receptacles.

38 A fire extinguisher should be visibly located in the kitchen, away from cooking equipment and 15" (38cm) to 48" (122cm) above the floor. Smoke alarms should be located near the kitchen.

39 The window/skylight area should equal at least 10 percent of the total square footage of the actual kitchen, or of the total living space which includes the kitchen (e.g., a kitchen within a family room).

40 Appropriate task and/or general lighting should illuminate every kitchen work surface.

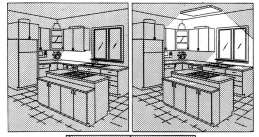

DIREC

ARCHITECTS & INTERIOR DESIGNERS

Architectural Artworks Inc.
Joan DesCombes
Roland DesCombes
163 East Morse Boulevard
Winter Park, Florida 32789
United States
Tel: (407) 644-1410
Fax: (407) 644-1016

Bruce Bierman
Bruce Bierman Design, Inc.
29 West 15th Street
New York, New York 10011
United States
Tel: (212) 243-1935
Fax: (212) 243-6615

Agnes Bourne, ASID
Agnes Bourne Studio
2 Henry Adams Street
San Francisco, California 94103
United States
Tel: (415) 626-6883
Fax: (415) 626-5914

Jane Brooks
Jane Brooks Interiors
1683 Shetland Place
Westlake Village, California 91362
United States
Tel: (805) 379-0042
Fax: (805) 373-5124

John A. Buscarello
John A. Buscarello, Inc.
27 West 20th Street, #1206
New York, New York 10011
United States
Tel: (212) 691-5881
Fax: (212) 691-5916

Carl D'Aquino Interiors, Inc.
Carl D'Aquino
Paul Laird
180 Varick Street
New York, NY 10014
United States
Tel: (212) 929-9787
Fax: (212) 929-9225

DiCicco Vinci · Ahn Architects
Carol DiCicco Vinci
James Ahn
135 Fifth Avenue
New York, New York 10010
United States
Tel: (212) 673-5495
Fax: (212) 673-5930

Mary Douglas Drysdale
Drysdale Design Associates
1733 Connecticut Avenue, N.W.
Washington, D.C. 20009
United States
Tel: (202) 588-0700
Fax: (202) 588-5086

Alexander Gorlin
Alexander Gorlin Architect
380 Lafayette Street
New York, New York 10003
United States
Tel: (212) 228-9000
Fax: (212) 254-8320

Johnny Grey
Johnny Grey and Company
Fyning Copse, Rogate
Petersfield, Hampshire GU 31 5DH
England
Tel: 01 730 821424
Fax: 01 730 821717

Cornelia Griffin
1930 Eddy Street
San Franciso, California 94115
United States
Tel: (415) 673-2773
Fax: (415) 673-5931

Paul Jacob Hill
Paul Jacob Hill Architects
80 Eighth Avenue, Suite 1010
New York, New York 10011
United States
Tel: (212) 206-7060
Fax: (212) 206-6322

Stephen Kinon, CKD
Ulrich Inc.
100 Chestnut Street
Ridgewood, New Jersey 07450
United States
Tel: (201) 445-1260
Fax: (201) 445-3552

James W. Krengel, CKD, CBD, IIDA
Kitchens By Krengel, Inc.
1688 Grand Avenue
St. Paul, Minnesota 55105
United States
Tel: (612) 698-0844
Fax: (612) 698-0683

TORY

L. Bogdanow & Associates Architects
Warren Ashworth
Randi Halpern
75 Spring Street
New York, New York 10012
United States
Tel: (212) 966-0313
Fax: (212) 941-8875

Eve Laron
Eve Laron Architects
18 Monash Avenue
2071 Killara
Sydney, New South Wales
Australia
Tel: 02 498 4187
Fax: 02 498 3543

Barton A. Lidsky
The Hammer and Nail, Inc.
232 Madison Avenue
Wyckoff, New Jersey 07481
United States
Tel: (201) 891-5252
Fax: (201) 891-0751

Arthur de Mattos Casas
Studio Arthur de Mattos Casas
Arquitetura Design
Alameda Ministro Rocha Azevedo 1052
São Paulo, São Paulo
Brazil 01410-002
Tel: 55 11 2826311
Fax: 55 11 2826608

Kristie Eagle McPhie, CKD
McPhie Cabinetry
436 East Main Street
Bozeman, Montana 59715
United States
Tel: (406) 586-1708
Fax: (406) 587-4353

Betsy Meyer, CKD, CBD
Betsy Meyer Associates, Inc.
P.O. Box 1179
Montauk Highway
Water Mill, New York 11976
United States
Tel: (516) 726-6428
Fax: (516) 726-6453

Robert Orr
Robert Orr & Associates (formerly Orr & Taylor)
441 Chapel Street
New Haven, Connecticut 06511
United States
Tel: (203) 777-3387
Fax: (203) 776-5684

McKee Patterson
Austin Patterson Associates
376 Pequot Avenue
Southport, Connecticut 06490
United States
Tel: (203) 255-4031
Fax: (203) 254-1390

Paul Bennett Architect
Paul Bennett
Phil Rutherford
22 West 21st Street, 12th floor
New York, New York 10010
United States
Tel: (212) 989-1313
Fax: (212) 989-8384

William C. Petrone
Sidnam Petrone Architects
136 West 21st Street
New York, New York 10011
United States
Tel: (212) 366-5500
Fax: (212) 366-6559

Paul Regan
Paul Regan, Architect
41 Union Square West
New York, New York 10003
United States
Tel: (212) 929-2831
Fax: (212) 633-1002

Reusser Bergstrom Associates
Marc Reusser
Debra Bergstrom
465 South El Molino Avenue, Suite 4
Pasadena, California 91101
United States
Tel: (818) 577-9088
Fax: (818) 577-1038

William Sofield
Studio Sofield
380 Lafayette Street
New York, New York 10003
United States
Tel: (212) 473-1300
Fax: (212) 473-0300

Mark D. Stumer
Mojo Stumer Associates
55 Bryant Avenue
Roslyn, New York 11576
United States
Tel: (516) 625-3344
Fax: (516) 625-3418

Angelo Tartaglia
Angelo Tartaglia Architect
Via Boezio 92 D9A
00192 Rome
Italy
Tel: 39 668 73879
Fax: 39 668 68449

Ilana Vardi
Kitchen Ideas Inc.
918 Route 22
North Plainfield, New Jersey 07060
United States
Tel: (908) 753-4141
Fax: (908) 755-6659

Colette Whitney
Whitney Interiors
537 Broadway
New York, New York 10012
United States
Tel: (212) 219-9654
Fax: (212) 219-9654

Peter Aprahamian
30 Nelson Road
London N89RU
England
Tel: 44 181 4824840
Fax: 44 181 4824849

Robert Vance Blosser
34 East 30th Street, Studio 25
New York, New York 10016
United States
Tel: (212) 679-2802
Fax: (212) 779-9281

Andrew Bordwin
70A Greenwich Avenue
New York, New York 10011
United States
Tel: (212) 633-0383
Fax: (212) 633-1046

Brian Vanden Brink
P.O. Box 419
Rockport, Maine 04856
United States
Tel: (207) 236-4035
Fax: (207) 236-0704

Frederick Charles
Frederick Charles Photography
254 Park Avenue South
New York, New York 10010
United States
Tel: (212) 505-0686
Fax: (212) 505-0692

Langdon Clay
511 Walnut Street
Sumner, Mississippi 38957
United States
Tel: (601) 375-7277

Dan Cornish
38 Evergreen Road
New Canaan, Connecticut 06840
United States
Tel: (203) 972-3714
Fax: (203) 972-1910

Grey Crawford
Grey Crawford Photography
2924 Park Center Drive
Los Angeles, California 90068
United States
Tel: (213) 413-4299
Fax: (213) 851-4252

Billy Cunningham
140 Sixth Avenue
New York, New York 10011
United States
Tel: (212) 929-6313
Fax: (212) 929-6318

Edoardo D'Antona
Via Montesanto 12
00195 Rome
Italy
Tel: 33 881 75218
Fax: 06 854 7980

Adrianne dePolo
18½ McKinley Street
Rowayton, Connecticut 06853
United States
Tel: (203) 838-3583
Fax: (203) 831-0349

Everett & Soulé
  Skip Everett
  Anne Soulé
P.O. Box 150674
Altamonte Springs, Florida 32715
United States
Tel: (407) 831-4183
Fax: (407) 831-4183

Roberta Frateschi
Roberta Frateschi Fotografa
Via Brisa 15
20123 Milan
Italy
Tel: 39 289 00402
Fax: 39 283 94007

Lizzie Himmel
50 West 29th Street, #12W
New York, New York 10001
United States
Tel: (212) 683-5331
Fax: (212) 725-3938

Christophe von Hohenberg
11 West 20th Street
New York, New York 10011
United States
Tel: (212) 677-2636
Fax: (212) 924-6215

Sergio Jorge
Jorge's Estudio
Rua Afons Freitas 432
São Paulo, São Paulo
Brazil 04006-052
Tel: 55 11 8878192

Andrew D. Lautman
Lautman Photography
4906 41st Street, N.W.
Washington, D.C. 20016
United States
Tel: (202) 966-2890
Fax: (202) 966-4240

Peter Ledwith
Peter Ledwith Photography
622 East 20th Street
New York, New York 10009
United States
Tel: (212) 228-1398

Jennifer Lévy
Jennifer Lévy Photography
245 West 29th Street
New York, New York 10001
United States
Tel: (212) 465-8684
Fax: (212) 564-8083

David Duncan Livingston
1036 Erica Road
Mill Valley, California 94941
United States
Tel: (415) 383-0898
Fax: (415) 383-0897

Peter Margonelli
524 Broadway, #605
New York, New York 10012
United States
Tel: (212) 941-0380
Fax: (212) 334-4449

Maytag Appliances
1 Dependability Square
Newton, Iowa 50208
United States
Tel: (515) 791-8711
Fax: (515) 781-8264

Jeff McNamara
68 Vista Drive
Easton, Connecticut 06612
United States
Tel: (203) 459-9175
Fax: (203) 459-9173

Jim Mims
Mims Photography
2281 Hampden Avenue
St. Paul, Minnesota 55114
United States
Tel: (612) 644-6488
Fax: (612) 644-4330

James Mortimer
15 Printing House Yard
Perserverence Works
Hackney Road
London E27NX
England
Tel: 44 171 7298858
Fax: 44 171 7298858

George Mott
51 Bank Street
New York, New York 10014
United States
Tel: (212) 242-2753

Michael Nicholson
49 Berry Road
2065 St. Léonard
New South Wales
Australia
Tel: 02 943 96539
Fax: 02 943 84413

Tuca Reinés
Tuca Reinés Estudio Fotografico
Rua Emanuel Kant 58
São Paulo, São Paulo
Brazil 04536-050
Tel: 55 11 30619127
Fax: 55 11 8528735

Laura Resen
29 Bethune Street
New York, New York 10014
United States
Tel: (212) 620-3153
Fax: (212) 727-0647

Peter Rymwid
47 Brighton Terrace
Wayne, New Jersey 07470
United States
Tel: (201) 628-1527
Fax: (201) 628-8897

Mark Samu
Samu Studios
P.O. Box 165
Bayport, New York 11705
United States
Tel: (516) 363-5902
Fax: (516) 363-5242

John Schwartz
77 Park Terrace East
New York, New York 10034
United States
Tel: (212) 567-9727

Everett Short
95 Christopher Street
New York, New York 10014
United States
Tel: (212) 255-9077
Fax: (212) 691-8661

Erik Unhjem
23 Golden Hill Avenue
Goshen, New York 10924
United States
Tel: (914) 294-3651

David Valenzuela
David Valenzuela Photography
1843 South Aprapahoe Street
Los Angeles, California 90006
United States
Tel: (213) 748-0644
Fax: (213) 748-7976

Roger Wade
Roger Wade Studio, Inc.
P.O. Box 1130
Condon, Montana 59826
United States
Tel: (406) 240-1066
Fax: (406) 754-3070

Wade Zimmerman
9 East 97th Street
New York, New York 10029-6925
United States
Tel: (212) 427-8784
Fax: (212) 427-3526

INDEX